Ghosts, Legends, and Lore of
Hampton Roads

Ghosts, Legends, and Lore of Hampton Roads

Cecilia
Petretto

Schiffer
Publishing Ltd ®

4880 Lower Valley Road, Atglen, Pennsylvania 19310

Dedication

For my mother, Sondra Ford Swift, whose spirit will always be my candle against the darkness. I love you and miss you.

Schiffer Books are available at special discounts for bulk purchases for sales promotions or premiums. Special editions, including personalized covers, corporate imprints, and excerpts can be created in large quantities for special needs. For more information contact the publisher:

Published by Schiffer Publishing Ltd.
4880 Lower Valley Road
Atglen, PA 19310
Phone: (610) 593-1777; Fax: (610) 593-2002
E-mail: Info@schifferbooks.com

For the largest selection of fine reference books on this and related subjects,
please visit our web site at:
www.schifferbooks.com
We are always looking for people to write books on new and related subjects.
If you have an idea for a book please contact us at the above address.

This book may be purchased from the publisher.
Include $5.00 for shipping.
Please try your bookstore first.
You may write for a free catalog.

In Europe, Schiffer books are distributed by
Bushwood Books
6 Marksbury Ave.
Kew Gardens
Surrey TW9 4JF England
Phone: 44 (0) 20 8392 8585; Fax: 44 (0) 20 8392 9876
E-mail: info@bushwoodbooks.co.uk
Website: www.bushwoodbooks.co.uk

Cover art: Ship © Jack Larmour. *Courtesy of www.bigstockphoto.com.*

Other Schiffer Books on Related Subjects
Haunted Virginia, 978-0-7643-3281-4, $14.99
Haunted Plantations of Virginia, 978-0-7643-3328-6, $14.99
Greetings from Hampton Roads, Virginia, 978-0-7643-2836-7, $34.99

Designed by Mark David Bowyer
Type set in Batik Regular / NewsGoth BT

ISBN: 978-0-7643-3426-9
Printed in the United States of America

Contents

Acknowledgments 6

Introduction 7

Section One: The Southside

Chapter One: Norfolk 22

Chapter Two: Virginia Beach and Chesapeake 29

Chapter Three: Portsmouth 51

Chapter Four: Suffolk 65

Chapter Five: The Great Dismal Swamp 73

Section Two: The Peninsula

Chapter Six: Hampton 84

Chapter Seven: Newport News 88

Chapter Eight: Gloucester 92

Chapter Nine: Williamsburg 93

Chapter Ten: Yorktown 99

Section Three: Ghosts, Legends, & Lore

Chapter Eleven: The Haunted Roads of Hampton Roads 110

Chapter Twelve: Other Haunted Places 122

Chapter Thirteen: The Legends of Hampton Roads 127

Afterword: A House on Holly Avenue 149

Bibliography 152

Index 158

Acknowledgments

Without the following contributions, this book would not have been possible:

† First I wish to thank Hampton Roads for being such an interesting and spooky place!

† Dinah Roseberry and my editor Jennifer Marie Savage for their guidance.

† Danny, my husband, who thought he'd never see the day I finished this project... I can now say to you that I am finished!

† My children, Jeremy, Melissa, and Shelby, whose tabs of mom doing the "ghost thing" cheered me up.

† My sister, Etain Swift... your ambition to succeed despite a series of setbacks has motivated me to do the same.

† My father, Dr. Donald Swift... your overwhelming support and professional advice allowed me to make wise choices.

† Jane Larish, my aunt... your own elegant prose has inspired my writing.

† To Kate Swift, my cousin... your energy and devotion to causes have inspired me.

† To Chris Maher... thank you so much for your spiritual advice and for being my mentor.

† To my family, friends, and colleagues... your encouragement got me through those difficult times.

† To the paranormal teams... your never-ending patience at my novice ability of ghost hunting, many questions, and sore feet was much appreciated.

† Lastly, thank you to all the people I interviewed for taking the time out of their busy schedules to speak to me.

Introduction

And as the moon from some dark gate
of cloud
Throws o'er the sea a floating bridge
of light,
Across whose trembling planks our fancies
crowd
Into the realm of mystery and night.
So from the world of spirits there descends
A bridge of light, connecting it with this,
O'er whose unsteady floor, that sways and
bends,
Wander our thoughts above the dark abyss.
— Henry Wadsworth Longfellow,
"Haunted Houses"

It is midnight and I'm in a cemetery hunting for ghosts.

In a setting straight out of an Edgar Allan Poe or a Stephen King story, the cemetery is dark and creepy as we carefully pick our way through. I see a cat...a black cat prowling between the tombstones. Our flashlights reflect its glowing eyes. It stares at us balefully before scampering away. An owl hoots nearby. A salient wind blows, almost mournfully, and the moon leers down at us. I keep expecting to see a skeletal hand poking out of a grave and pointing at me. Somebody cue the spooky music.

"What was that?" I asked, looking fearfully about.

At least I'm not alone. My companion-in-arms is Kayla from a local ghost hunting team, the Lakeland Skeptics Society. They are a group of high school students led by Earth Science teacher Marcus Daniels that investigates ghosts using the scientific method. She seems wiser than her fifteen years as she explains the function and importance of her equipment in relation to her work.

We're in Yorktown, Virginia, in a very historical area dotted with centuries-old houses and a nearby battleground where American forces fought against the British in an effort to gain independence in the late eighteenth century. The area is also reputed to be haunted, and the graveyard we are in contains markers dating back one hundred years.

"Nothing. Just me," she reasons. Of course *she* is calm, cool, and rational. The team's credo is that the most obvious and simplest observation is often the correct one.

We then hear sounds as if someone or something is yelling, but we rationally identify the voice as one of a drunken reveler. The ghost hunting expedition happened to coincide with a very noisy and crowded event at a nearby park. The drunk is walking away (the event had ended), leaving us in peace. Kayla places an EMF (electromagnetic field) meter on one tombstone while I take pictures with my digital camera. An EMF gives specific readings of electromagnetic energies (Warren, 2003). Suddenly the device lights up. We stare at it. We're in a graveyard, she reminds me, there shouldn't be any electronic interference. Did we just receive a "call" from the nether world? Did a presence just temporarily manifest itself? A chill descends along my spine.

Okay, I'm getting jumpy, but this is a graveyard, and I'm not sure what I'll do if I do encounter a ghost. I am not a ghost hunter. I am a writer. All I know about ghost hunting is from the paranormal TV programs I've watched from the safety of my living room. Usually the question of the haunting is easily answered by the end of the show. The participants of the show spend much of the time probing the unknown with various gadgets and flashlights against the dramatic effect of the night. The media savvy ghost hunter is oftentimes akin to the detective of film noir or a maverick as he strives to solve the mystery by the end of the show (Brogan, 1998/Weinstock, 2004). The ghosts are arguably the liability. What is missing from these shows, as any paranormal investigator will tell you, is the actual work the investigation involves. It is not limited to just the investigation of the a haunted site, but the hours and hours of listening to tapes, conducting interviews and research, viewing film footage, and determining the results from the equipment. Usually the investigations at a site are hours long, sometimes taking several days or nights, and the exhausting work may yield very little by way of lack of evidence. I was fortunate enough to be able to accompany a ghost hunting team on one investigation and I interviewed others about their experiences — many are quite the intrepid type, wanting to explain the unseen world rather than fear it.

A recent Gallup Poll survey shows that thirty-two percent of those surveyed believe in ghosts, forty-one percent believe in ESP, and twenty-one percent in psychic ability. Iconic movies such as "Ghostbusters" and "Ghost," TV and cable shows such as "The Ghost Whisperer," "Ghost Hunters," and even children's shows such as "Danny Phantom" reveal how much the paranormal has mainstreamed into popular culture (Black, 2007). Books by the thousands offer practical approaches and advice on how to hunt ghosts and classes in ghost hunting can be found on the Internet. Even some college composition courses are integrating the method to allow critical thinking (Ibid). Yet ghosts represent the unknown, the intangible, and the unexplained. Novels, television, and especially Hollywood take advantage of our fear of ghosts, creating celluloid fiends that stalk helpless teenagers, a very profitable endeavor. As mostly rational folk, we are quick to explain strange phenomenon with logic and reason, but the fear lurks in our unconscious. Those who, after being alone in a dark, creepy place at night, hear or see something unusual are usually loathe to discuss it because of the possibility of not being believed. We struggle for reasonable explanations, but the fear, rising from the depths of our consciousness like specters, paralyzes us with dread. However, the fear of ghosts can be considered as childish and silly, which is ironic given that most of our fears stem from childhood. The belief in ghosts as a child often rendered me helpless, as I would lay awake, hearing a sound and seeing something move in my opened closet. I would cry out to my parents, who would stumble in my room, half awake and greatly annoyed, to reassure me that, "*There are no such things as* **ghosts**!" They would then make me promise not to read scary comic books before bed, but as soon as they turned off my bedroom light and left, the noises reoccurred...as did glimpses of the "Closet Ghoul."

To this day I still cannot sleep with an open closet, and I'm careful not to let any appendages dangle when in bed. I also remember the nightly ghost stories at summer camp. The heat of the campfire that we gathered around felt hot against my face, but the counselors' stories would give me the chills. During sleep-overs, my girlfriends and I would try to scare each other silly with ghost stories to stave off sleep, only to collapse into an exhausted heap at dawn, troubled by junk food induced nightmares. As I grew older, my childish fears of ghosts were replaced by tangible fears that adulthood unfortunately had in ample supply: bills, parenting, and work. Yet ghosts have always fascinated me, whether by the discovery of a place that is haunted, people's experience with ghosts, or the scientific investigation of a haunting.

The ghost stories I heard growing up and have collected over the years have different names — the Lady in White, the Ghostly Hitchhiker, the Bog Man, the Screaming Skull — but most have similar themes: justice or revenge, betrayal, and murder brought on by intense hatred or unrequited love. The motifs are similar too: apparitions of young women in white who wait for lovers that never come, eerie lights that bob and flicker, mysterious bloodstains that never fade, glowing red eyes in the dark, and the disembodied cries and sobs of grief. Some ghosts bring the elements of their demise: the dampness, seaweed, or puddles associated with drowning, for example, or the bloodied footprint. Most ghost stories have a moral, or told as a parable, that teaches us proper behavior. However, an actual ghost sighting or experience may have some or none of these elements. Most ghost sightings are personal and do not offer any guidance or messages. It is usually up to the beholder to ascertain just what the ghost wants, which can be quite the challenge.

I have never seen a ghost, but I have experienced something similar. I was seventeen and vacationing with my family in Maine. I was with my sister Etain and her then-husband. Out of boredom, we decided to get away from the confines of the family cabin and do a little bit of driving along the coast. Most of coastal Maine is lush with thick forests, rocky beaches, and quaint villages. Maine is also renowned for fog that rolls over the forest like a primeval blanket, casting even the most familiar wooded paths as labyrinthine and mysterious.

Along the way, we stopped at a charming country church that dated back a couple of hundred years and which had an extensive cemetery in the back. Compelled by morbid fascination, we alighted from the car and made our way past recent headstones lined along the front of the cemetery to the older ones in the back. I became separated from the others as I picked my way through, trying to avoid stepping on the actual graves. I stopped at a few, wondering who the departed were and what sense and stance they had made in the world; some persons, such as children and women, were only in existence for such a short while. I passed others, and realized how many had died in such quantities and in such a short time. My macabre fascination slid into sadness as I pondered the harshness of the early colonial settlements and how incredibly fast disease could reduce the village's population in a matter of days.

I remember standing there at the farthest edge of the cemetery. It was getting late. I looked for my sister and her husband and saw that they had begun to head back to the car. Etain looked at me and gestured at her watch. I waved back, but decided to linger a moment or two to take a couple of pictures. As I took them I abruptly noticed that the bird song from the forest around the cemetery had ceased. I felt cold, but then again it was getting late in the afternoon and the sun's bright rays were becoming diminished by the thickening tendrils of fog blowing in from the nearby sea, very typical of that region of coastal Maine. Then I heard a faint sound...a muffled sound. I stopped and looked around, but found no one. I heard it again... this time it was distinct, as if someone was calling out from underground. I again peered over the headstones and saw figures of my sister and her husband dwindling in the distance as they headed for the car. The fog was really becoming thick, so thick that I could no longer see anything but the headstones around me. I felt watched, yet there was no one around, and I felt scared, *very* scared. I felt as if a bodiless presence was regarding me and its intentions were hostile. I called out, but my voice was a feeble croak. I called again and did not hear anything.

Quickly, I headed back to what I thought were the obscured outlines of the church, but only encountered a small crypt. Realizing the reduction of visibility and the possibility that I was lost, I began to panic. The presence around me was becoming stronger. I broke into a run, and as I ran I felt that I was leaving the presence behind me. I stumbled, getting mud all over my knees and almost losing my camera, but quickly got up to continue my fleeing. After what seemed like an eternity, I blessedly saw the church finally looming up out of the fog. As I made my way back to the car, my sister looked askance at my disheveled appearance and remarked how pale I looked. Her husband joked that I must have seen a ghost. Not wanting them to think anything, I mumbled that I got lost in the fog and had a difficult time trying to find my way back. As I got in the car, I hid my fear as best I could. My hands were shaking, so I stuffed them in my jacket pockets. As we drove away, I looked back at the church; the view of it was almost completely obliterated by the fog, and I wondered what had just happened to me. Did I encounter a ghost? Or was it just my imagination?

Being the conscientious offspring of a scientist allowed me a rational approach to all things unseen and hard to prove that usually provided me with answers. I have explored every conceivable explanation. I was a very sensitive seventeen year old, prone to a fanciful imagination, much of it fostered by the likes of such writers as Edgar Allan Poe, Emily Bronte, Shirley Jackson, and Stephen King, who uses the eerie side of Maine as the setting in many of his novels. When I was a child, my mother, a lover of regional legends and folktales, would regale me with colorful fairy and ghost stories. "The Exorcist" scared the bejeebers out of me when I was a kid, as did the popular slasher movies of the 1980s: "Friday the 13th," "Nightmare on Elm Street," and "Halloween." In addition, being alone in a fog-shrouded cemetery would allow almost anyone's imagination to run amok. Perhaps the muffled sound I heard was from the caretaker, whom I had seen there. Perhaps his voice was made askew by the echo of the gravestones. But rational explanation falls short by the photographs I took. What was really troubling is the film I tried to develop of that cemetery did not come out. The two photos I took of those headstones were dark and blurry. The rest of the film came out fine, except for those two pictures. And that unspeakable terror I felt in the presence of something or someone seemingly not of this earth is something I cannot explain.

To this day I still do not know what happened to me. I have used every angle of every scientific, logical explanation of this experience, but have come to no conclusion. The feeling of being stalked that drove me this close to fear is something that I never want to experience again. I have passed that same church and cemetery countless times since then, as my family still frequents the same cabin every summer, and I still have no desire to revisit that place again.

Typically, most people's experiences with a haunting are by decade's old or even hundred-year-old ghosts, but some claim to be haunted by familiar ghosts, even recently deceased relatives. For example, a friend of my husband's, Aaron, lived in a townhouse in Virginia Beach with his then-wife. After a few months of residing in the house, they began experiencing strange occurrences. It began subtly: sudden temperature drops in various parts of the house, feelings of someone brushing by when no one was around, and lights flickering on and off, or lights being on when Aaron distinctly remembered turning them off. However, the incidents began to occur more frequently and were becoming increasingly more bizarre, even downright scary. Aaron recalls one incident in which he and his wife had returned home to find an interesting mess. As a countertop decoration in the kitchen, they had a plastic fruit display complete with bananas, apples, oranges, and grapes. Aaron discovered that someone had methodically removed each of the plastic grapes and had thrown them about all over the counter and floor. The strangest experience was an encounter between the presence and his two-year-old stepdaughter. Aaron happened upon her playing in the kitchen. He thought nothing of it when she began to prattle away to no one in particular, spinning a yarn of an adventure about her favorite doll. But when it seemed as though she was answering questions and was addressing someone, he began to become alarmed. When he asked her who she was speaking to, she answered, "The man." Other times their cat would react to something that they couldn't see or hear. Once, the cat was sleeping peacefully on the couch. Quite suddenly, the cat leapt into the air, yowling and hissing. Fur on its body standing on end, it scampered away still growling. It hid under the bed and would not come out until his wife coaxed it out with an offer of sardines. He and his wife would experience a pall of negative energy that would descend over the house. He would describe the feeling the minute he walked into the house as something so bad and touched with despair that he and his wife immediately felt terrible. The feeling would subside when they left the dwelling.

Feeling anxious, he and his wife discussed their experiences, called some family members, and soon learned what was haunting their home. Aaron describes one encounter that explained their whole experience. They were sitting in the living room; his wife in a rocker and he was sitting opposite from her and could see into the kitchen. The conversation thread weaved in and out of problems with relatives until it wound around the subject of his wife's deceased grandfather. The grandfather had been dead for two years, but apparently made life very difficult for relatives, particularly for Aaron's wife. Nobody got along with the man. As she sat in her rocking chair, his wife and her sisters discussed their relationship with the grandfather while Aaron sat quietly by them. He caught something out of the corner of his eye. In the kitchen, a very heavy tall glass was in the dish drainer. Before his eyes it began to tremble and then lift in the air. It arced high above the sink and then smashed onto the adjacent counter, splintering glass everywhere. Everybody, startled at the sound, ran into the kitchen and viewed the wreckage. It all came together: the unexplained experiences, the cat's reaction, and most of all his stepdaughter's strange conversation — it was the wife's grandfather, a man whom she and her family did not easily get along with, that explained the negative feelings.

The grandfather had no apparent connection to the townhouse. He never lived at the townhouse, for he had died before they had even moved in. After the glass incident, the disturbances gradually declined until they stopped altogether. Since then none of them have been affected by the grandfather's ghost. Why the grandfather was distant to the granddaughter yet so close to her after his death can be explained in that perhaps he was making amends of their relationship, or that the connection between them was so strong he couldn't break it...even after his death.

Sometimes a haunting doesn't consist of one ghost and the usual activity of doors opening on their own accord and the sound of disembodied footsteps. Sometimes an area or house can be affected with a massive supernatural influence...almost a collective haunting by many ghosts. My husband experienced such a haunting. He is a carpenter and was at a job site that was a centuries-old house. My husband is a thorough worker, and often is the last to leave. One day, Danny was working late at the site. The owners were on vacation while the work was being done, so he was alone. It was one of the cool autumn days and the air was so still you could hear a dog barking a mile away. Although it was only a little after six, the sun had nearly set and stars began to appear in the twilight sky. He heard the sound faintly at first... the sound of children playing. Shouts of glee, laughing, and sing-song chants as if a group of children were nearby. He looked around, but couldn't see anyone. The owners were an elderly couple and were away. Perhaps it was a daycare facility close by, he shrugged, and the sounds he heard were carried over by the cold dense air. He went back to work, but the sounds became louder and clearer as wave after wave of children's noises rolled over him and echoed off the house. The sound was so loud that he could hear each child's voice and could determine that there were many of them, maybe six or seven boys and girls, and that they were playing an old game of kick-the-can that his grandfather used to tell him about. Then, as gradually as the sounds first became evident, they faded away as if he was driving out of the range of a radio station. He wasn't unnerved by the incident, just curious as to what the sounds may be and how they were caused. Later, he discovered that the sounds were a common occurrence, for the house used to have servants' quarters in the back. The dwelling had a rather large family, eight children, and the children used to play between it and the main house. Tragedy had befallen the family. Yellow fever claimed the mother and the children, but the father survived. The father couldn't bear the pain any longer and subsequently died a year later of a broken heart. The children were often described as jovial and full of energy and used to play, since they had no other toys, kick-the-can.

Ghosts fall into two categories: remnants and those who are conscious of the living. Remnants are ghosts who are trapped between two worlds, as they are often not aware that they have died. Some are victims of violent crimes. A haunting of this type seem unaware of those who behold them (residual), as if stuck in whatever they were doing at time of death, completely oblivious to those who see it. Usually the haunting involves the ghost finishing whatever business he/she needs on this plane before moving onto the next. Other hauntings involve ghosts who are aware of their surroundings (intelligent) and can, at times, to make life miserable for the living. Poltergeists fall in another category: this haunting is usually dangerous and destructive at worst or a nuisance by misplacing objects or making noise at best. Usually poltergeist activity is a short duration haunting. Then there are those who have beheld an apparition, with some people seeing a full-bodied apparition, although he or she may never wish to do so again. Children and adolescents tend to be ghost sensitive. Some are more attuned than others, almost as if having antennas that probe wavelengths of higher pitch, while others may just feel an uncertainty about them, never really seeing something but definitely feeling it.

Throughout this book, I use "ghost" and "spirit" frequently. While some argue that there is a distinction between the two, others do not. The argument is more connotative than denotative. If we were to argue the meaning, we should look at the etymology, which is the study of the word given its structure and origin. The word ghost is derived from Middle English *ghast* (i.e., ghastly), which is traced back to Old High German (Anglo Saxon) *geist* (ghost), and means either an imprint of human form or intelligence left behind after the death of an individual. The word *spirit* is Middle English, presumably Latin *spiritus* (breath) and *spirare*, which means to breathe. The word *spirit* means the animating force that exists in a living being or can exist after death (i.e., living breath; to medieval thinkers this meant the soul; as in when dying, the soul departs the body with the last breath). These concepts' meaning can even be affected by region and culture, similar to *spigot* versus *faucet* if I were to argue semantics. The meanings are arguably similar; both words mean a force that exists after the physical body no longer functions. This energy can be intelligent of its situation or bereft of any knowledge of its existence as it continues to go through the daily motions it once did when alive or during the time of death (i.e., murder is often the case). Therefore, although some may vehemently disapprove, I will use the two concepts interchangeably.

This book invites you to come along and experience places around Hampton Roads that are purported to be haunted and to delve into the mystery of the haunting. I have been living in Hampton Roads, Virginia, since 1986 and I would like to share its rich history. The interviews I have conducted with those who have witnessed apparitions, experienced hauntings, or investigate the paranormal shed light on various perspectives of ghosts. Over the years, I have collected popular ghost lore of the region that suggests various recurrent motifs often found in other locales.

As an added feature, I have included a chapter about the legends, dead and living, of Hampton Roads and their lasting impact on the region. As a treat, I also included some urban legends, always entertaining, that have enhanced local folklore. This book is a narrative of the places I've been and people I've interviewed. I hope that you will find these places as interesting and engaging as I have. Perhaps you'll decide to visit one of the places mentioned and experience it for yourself... maybe even encounter a ghost!

Ghosts in Hampton Roads? Maybe. I'll leave that up to you.

Courtesy of the *Suffolk Department of Economic Development* (www.suffolk.va.us).

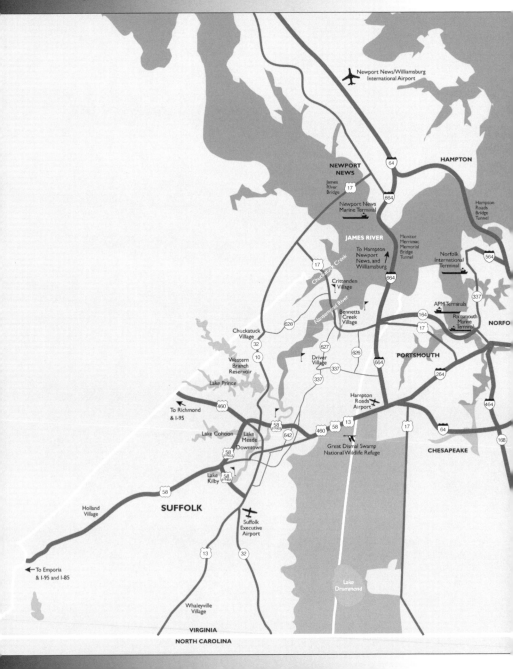

About Hampton Roads

Many of my out-of-state relatives and friends have always puzzled over the name Hampton Roads. Perhaps because they often associate "Roads" as the major Interstate, avenues, boulevards, and other asphalt-paved thoroughfares that carry traffic in and out of the area. However, the name Hampton Roads actually represents the area's proximity to the tidal estuaries that are a vast network of waterways (i.e., tidewater). One cannot travel twenty miles in any direction without going over a body of water. The name also signifies the colonists' early dependency on the rivers for livelihood. Plantations and settlements were built along the Elizabeth, James, and York Rivers. The Chesapeake Bay links these rivers to the Atlantic Ocean (Salmon, 2007). These waterways made transporting goods easier than on land. Most of the estates' income was from ships that frequented the area.

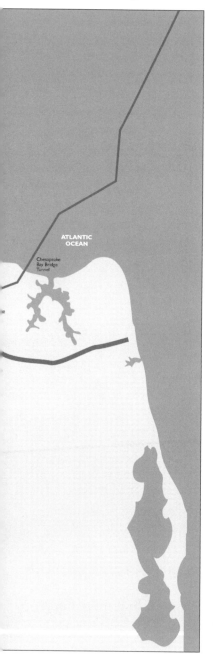

The name is a nautical term of roadstead: "a sheltered body of water that is not quite a harbor, in which ships may ride at anchor" (Ibid). The moniker was first established by early English colonists who had to defend their outposts throughout the area from pirates and hostile Native American tribes. The term Hampton referred to the area that was named after the Earl of Southampton by the first royal governor, Lord de la Ware. The Earl was a major investor of the Virginia Company of London, which primarily funded the exploration and colonization (Virginia's Hampton Roads, 2009). Eventually Southampton was shortened to Hampton, and as the area grew to include the cities of Virginia Beach, Norfolk, Portsmouth, Chesapeake, Suffolk, Hampton, Newport News, Yorktown, and Williamsburg it became Greater Hampton Roads.

The area is rich in history. Although various tribes of Native Americans had inhabited the land long before the arrival of English settlers, Jamestown colonists, led by the legendary John Smith, were among the first citizens of America in the early seventeenth century. Despite various setbacks from hostile encounters with the Powhatans, droughts, disease, and famine, this small settlement grew into a prosperous community. By mid-eighteenth century Virginia's population tripled. The colonies flourished. Williamsburg became the first capital of the burgeoning nation in 1699. Tobacco production had made land owners very wealthy, and created vast estates along the James and York Rivers. By the end Revolutionary War in 1783, famous Virginians such as George Washington and Thomas Jefferson helped create an independent nation free from the power struggles early American colonists had with Britain. Later, during the Civil War, great battles were again fought along the Peninsula in cities such as Hampton, Newport News, and Yorktown. Still, during the years of World War II, German submarines stalked the coastal waters off Virginia Beach (The Encyclopedia of Virginia, 1999).

Hampton Roads is a cornucopia of legend and lore. Many legends have enhanced the history of the area. Pirates such as Blackbeard wreaked havoc along the coast of Virginia Beach. Grace Sherwood, accused of witchcraft, was tried and convicted in the late seventeenth century and then later pardoned by Governor Gilmore three hundred years later. Famous living figures such as Dr. Madblood lends more local flavor to the mix. Perhaps because Hampton Roads is the oldest area in the state of Virginia, it is known to be haunted. Sightings of ghosts rambling through crumbling antebellum mansions, spirits caught in a long ago time still linger in historic homes, and tragic events such as the brutality of slavery have left a lasting impression on the living all make Hampton Roads historically significant. But the ghosts of Hampton Roads are not limited to historical sites. Death is indiscriminate. One does not have to be famous to be a ghost. Emotional turmoil can leave an imprint on a place. Some everyday suburban houses are reputed to be haunted as are hotels, roads, hospitals, and of course cemeteries. Even these places offer a unique history of their own.

Whether or not you believe in ghosts, you will find that Hampton Roads is an area worthy of interest, and possibly a visit.

Section One:

The Southside

Norfolk ~ Virginia Beach/Chesapeake ~ Portsmouth ~ Suffolk ~ the Great Dismal Swamp

The area south of the James River and west of the Chesapeake Bay — the two major waterways that share the Hampton Roads — is known as the Southside or Southern Hampton Roads. It's a region located in the extreme southeastern portion of Virginia and made up of the cities Norfolk, Portsmouth, Virginia Beach, Chesapeake, and Suffolk.

At one time, the Southside was a separate region from the Peninsula. The James River Bridge spanned Route 17 across James River to the county of Isle of Wight, establishing the only connection from Richmond to Portsmouth and Norfolk. The residents of Hampton or Newport News had to travel to Norfolk or Virginia Beach by ferry. It wasn't until the mid-1970s that the Hampton Roads Bridge Tunnel was built to connect these two regions. Despite the access, most residents of the Southside still consider the region distinctive than the rest.

Chapter One

Norfolk

With all its Southern charm and appeal, Norfolk's ghosts are legendary.

> The spirit-world around this world of sense
> Floats like an atmosphere, and everywhere
> Wafts through these earthly mists and vapors dense
> A vital breath of more ethereal air.
> — Henry Wadsworth Longfellow,
> "Haunted Houses"

The Moses Myers House...

Feeling a Presence

On Bank Street, the Moses Myers House was built by a prosperous businessman, Moses Myers, for his family between 1792 and 1797. It is one of the first brick houses built after the destruction wreaked by the British during the Revolutionary War. Moses was a prominent citizen in a thriving Jewish community, and he and his wife Eliza raised their family in the house. After Moses Myers' death in 1835, over five generations of the Myers family lived in the Moses Myers House until it eventually became a museum in the 1930s.

The house is reputed to be haunted.

According to *The Virginian-Pilot*, Samantha Weaver, an interpreter and garden historian at the house from 1995 to 2006, claims to have seen a specter of a man in the garden (Zirckle, 2008). He is reported to be wearing a top hat and cloak and is seen pacing restlessly back and forth with his hands clasped behind his back. Allegedly, the man was shot by Samuel Myers, Moses son. Apparently, Moses Myers and his partner in business, Thomas Bowden, were debating over a loan, which quickly escalated into a heated argument. Bowden hit Myers in the face. Later after cooling down and resting inside the house, Myers recovered. However, things went awry when Samuel mistakenly became involved and impulsively shot Bowden with a pistol. Legal proceedings resulted in Samuel's innocence. Bowden is forever trapped in the garden because he never lived at the house, according to Weaver.

Inside the house, three generations of the Myers family are said to still walk the halls. I interviewed Vivian Washington, a former employee who felt the presence of the spirits that call the house home. She started working at the house during the summer of 1992 as a costumed tour guide. Normally she didn't see "things" other than the usual tourist who visited the house. She worked various morning, afternoon, and evening shifts, sometimes staying late for special events. Two parts of the house made her feel uneasy: the attic and the basement. She described the attic as storage for artifacts and linens, and the basement being a bookstore. Between tours she would occasionally practice her walkthroughs. On several occasions, she said, she had a feeling that she was not alone in the house. She describes the feeling as "not scary, just an uneasiness... I would feel uneasy at the top of the house."

"Did you feel cold?" I asked her.

"It mainly felt like someone was watching me," she said. "Not like movement...just watching me."

Indeed, the second floor is where most of the activity occurs. Four Myers children of various ages passed away in the house, including Adeline, Moses's daughter.

"Most people think they see the oldest daughter, because she was engaged to be married and she never loved any other man," Weaver said. "It's true that I feel her presence."

Two of Moses's sons died, and later his wife died, possibly due to the heartbreak of losing her sons. Moses eventually met his demise in 1835 in the very same bed that can be viewed today. People have reported seeing an indentation of someone's head on the pillow and a form outlining a person's body in the bed.

Others report seeing a little girl both in and outside the house. Blonde and always dressed in loose-fitting dress, she appears mostly in the evenings in an upstairs bedroom. She reportedly never acknowledges those who behold her...she just smiles and vanishes into thin air.

Who would ever want to spend the night in such a spooky place? A bunch of teenagers, that's who! On October 3, 2008, a group of high school students decided to brave the eerie reputation of the house by spending the night...not to conduct a paranormal investigation, but to report on what they experienced for the local paper. A security guard and the manager of historic houses were on hand to chaperone the group. First, the group whetted their appetites by learning about the ghostly history of the place. They then prepared to stay up all night in hopes of encountering spooks. The night turned out to be rather eventful, for at several places in the house the teenagers felt watched and experienced drops in temperature. Later, right before dawn, one teen named Morgan described seeing something like a nebulous manifestation that floated near her and then disappeared. "I'm not saying it's a ghost, but it was enough to make me think that maybe there are ghosts and maybe they're in the house." (Ibid)

Ghosts at the Moses Myers House? There could very well be.

The Freemason Abbey Restaurant...

Offering More Than Great Food

For over twenty years, an evening without dining at the Freemason Abbey Restaurant was a dull night indeed. According to the restaurant's website, the Freemason Abbey was originally a church in 1873. In 1902, the congregation of Second Presbyterian Church sold the property to the First Church of Christ Scientist, which occupied the building until 1948. From 1948 through 1987, it served as a meeting hall for the Independent Order of Odd Fellows. In the late 1980s, the Freemason Abbey Restaurant & Tavern became a familiar landmark to historical downtown Norfolk.

This elegant yet very affordable eatery offers a wide range of menu choices. Although not listed on the menu, there is allegedly a ghost.

I spoke to one of the staff members, who, on the condition of anonymity, described experiencing a temperature drop in the pantry and the feeling that someone had brushed up against her in the kitchen, but nobody was around. Reports of strange activity such as straws being knocked out of glasses, cooks' apron strings being untied, cupboard doors opening on their own accord, and employees noticing dried goods and cans being moved around or knocked over in the pantry was enough to get one paranormal team, Hampton Roads Paranormal Society (HaRPS), interested. In between investigations, I had the opportunity to interview several members of the team.

Kristine James, founder and lead investigator, explained to me that HaRPS' motto is a scientific approach to what goes bump in the night and that her team is truly dedicated and professional. She is careful to point out that a site reported to be allegedly haunted may not actually be haunted. What is believed to be paranormal activity might be the result of faulty electrical wiring, extraneous noise, vibration from nearby construction sites or traffic, or even an overactive imagination. Kristine argues, "Anybody can have a 'feeling', especially if the person has been told the place is haunted prior to experiencing something."

Corrie Shumate, another investigator, adds that a couple of sites reputed to be haunted were investigated by his team, but yielded little to nothing in terms of paranormal activity because of these factors. As with any professional paranormal team, all findings are thoroughly reviewed before making any formal conclusion. When I asked her about the TV paranormal shows that often include an easy ending with the ghost bagged and tagged, Kristine comments, "It's not a glamorous job. We are not in this for the glory. We are here to help."

The paranormal activity was thought to be caused by the former owner. The team investigated the restaurant in May 2008. They arrived at the restaurant after closing because they didn't want to interfere with their business operation, and met with the manager. After a tour and overview of the activity, the technical team set up base in the office while employees of the restaurant were interviewed about their experiences. One of the areas they wished to investigate was the bar, where, according to accounts, straws had been removed from glasses. After the manager, wait staff, and kitchen employees left for the night, the team settled down for what they hoped to be a quiet night. Hours passed and they didn't think they were going to find anything. However, their evidence included an EVP recording of a woman crying and a mysterious photograph. A report from their website describes their experience:

At about 3 a.m. investigators monitoring the video cameras watched in astonishment as the straws in the glass placed on the bar began to move! We quickly radioed the investigators currently in the bar to confirm the activity. Those monitoring the cameras were then informed from a very punchy investigation team that they were the culprits. This is an example of keeping levity in situations where the hour is late and the monitors inactive. It is things like this that keep us alert throughout our long vigils.

"An anomalous shadow" was also photographed. Corrie describes the shadow as a black figure — *a silhouette* — with its arm resting on its leg. The figure was moving when it was taken. As their website report concludes, "Comparing this to photographs taken prior to lights out, we ascertained that the shadow was not caused by light reflection or other objects present in the room. We could find no explanation for this shadow."

As of this writing, the team feels that their findings are inconclusive, for the photograph does not yield the evidence they feel is necessary for their investigation to be definitive of paranormal activity. They feel another investigation — maybe two or three more investigations — is necessary before making a formal conclusion that Freemason Abbey is haunted. Corrie maintains the team's stance on the scientific method: "We need something solid."

Although the jury is still out on whether or not the Freemason Abbey is actually haunted, reports of strange goings-on in the kitchen and bar area are still being posted in paranormal chat rooms on the Internet. As I mentioned, paranormal investigation is not an exact science, and it takes a few investigations to actually yield conclusive results. If you are planning a visit to the Freemason Abbey Restaurant, perhaps you will experience an eerie sensation of something not of this world...or at least excellent dining.

Nauticus Museum in Norfolk offers a ghost tour that includes Freemason Abbey. The tour is called Sea Legends and Ghosts: A Downtown Walkaround. Call 664-1000 for more information.

Opposite Page:
The Freemason Abbey Restaurant

Norfolk's Other Haunted Places

Norfolk County Jail

This is a great story. In one cell, a man clings to the desperate hope that his sentence will be light even though he had committed murder. Burdened by his shame and guilt, he hanged himself. Years later, another man looks into the mirror, but he does not see his reflection. Rather he sees ghostly features that are not his. As he sleeps, he feels something cold touch his arm during the night. Another night, his blankets are ripped from him. Soon, other men who had stayed in the same cell experience similar happenings, and reports of the cell still being haunted have circulated the Internet.

The Page House Inn

The mother of the Inn's owner is said to haunt the place. Every once in a while her dining room china cabinet opens and shuts. Other reports include doors opening and closing on their own accord and the sound of footsteps in the middle of the night.

St. Paul's Church

This is quite possibly the oldest church in the area. After Lord Dunmore, the last British governor of Virginia, bombarded Norfolk January 1, 1776, a cannonball became lodged in the wall...and remains there to this day. Several specters inhabit this church and a mysterious figure prowls the graveyard. Others say the ghost of a long dead priest still keeps vigil over the church.

The Ghost of Willoughby Spit

Similar to the South Carolina legend of the Gray Man, the ghost of Willoughby Spit in the Ocean View section of Norfolk portends hurricanes. The Spit was formed by a hurricane in the late eighteenth century. A man and his family had died in the storm. Locals say he only appears before a hurricane hits as a solitary figure walking along the shoreline. His ghost has appeared twice: before an unnamed hurricane in the 1920s and before Hurricane Isabel in 2003. Forecasters say that Hampton Roads is overdue for a major hurricane. Only the ghost of Willoughby Spit knows when it will be.

Chapter Two:
Virginia Beach and Chesapeake

Virginia Beach Haunts

Despite its popularity as a beach resort and extensive list of fun things to do, Virginia Beach has its share of ghosts.

~~~~~

The Ferry Plantation House

Off the Western Branch of the Lynnhaven River stands the Ferry Plantation House. The house got its name because it was near the many tidal waterways that were accessible to ferries, the means of transportation two hundred years ago (Yarsinske, 2002). Prior to this site was the first brick courthouse for Princess Anne County, where Grace Sherwood, the legendary Witch of Pungo, was tried. Anthony Walke purchased the land about 1770, but the house wasn't built until the early 1800s. The Walkes were a prestigious family in early Virginia Beach history, and they were part of the elite planter class that held political sway over the region between 1715 and 1745 (Mansfield, 1989). It was an era known for its prosperity that was built upon the tobacco trade and slave labor. The first Anthony Walke served in the House of Burgesses. In 1787, the second Anthony Walke and his cousin, Thomas Walke IV, were among the delegates who participated in Virginia's ratification of the Constitution; Virginia being the tenth state to do so. Walke II later served in the Virginia legislature before moving to Ohio (Yarsinske, 2002). Not only was Walke II involved with the business of politics, but he enjoyed merriment as well. An archaeological dig near the Ferry House yielded the remains of a tavern owned by him in 1770, which was later left it to his son, William. The manor house burned down in 1828, but was not rebuilt until 1830 by later descendents of the Walke family, Elizabeth Mason Walke and her husband George McIntosh (Ibid). Because of its desired locale and rich farmland, it has been a popular house as it was sold too many families over the past two hundred years. It has withstood the passage of time, including the War of 1812 and the Civil War, a silent witness to the ever-changing face of the South. It then stood empty for a number of years during the 1980s until Friends of Ferry Plantation House began the long task of restoring and maintaining the house (Barrow, 1996). It is now a museum that offers guided tours, including haunted tours. For more information, visit the site's website at www.ferryplantation.org.

What ghosts precisely walk the halls of the Ferry Plantation House have been debated, but speculation is that they don't rest easy. The Ferry Plantation House offers spirit tours. I recommend going more than once. You are allowed to do your own paranormal investigating after the tour is finished as long as you comply with the regulations (i.e., no access after 10 p.m., no damage to the house, and no unlawful entry). I went on two of the haunted tours: the first to get a feel for the house and the second to gain what I had missed the first time. One evening during the summer, I parked my van in the small parking area and gazed at the house. It is an immense brick, two-story colonial, looking more like a historical house found in Colonial Williamsburg. Indeed, the house stands so incongruously to the more modern structures of the rather affluent subdivision that surrounds it. As the sun sank in the west and we began the tour, I was determined to find out about the ghosts.

Second Floor Haunts

The second floor of the house is where the most active haunting takes place. A descendent of the Walke family, Sally Rebecca, is one of the many ghosts that still reside in the house. During the Civil War, one cool spring night in April 1863, six female cousins of the Walke family, including Sally, huddled in the house, fearing for their husbands, brothers, and male friends involved in battle. Upstairs by the fireplace, Sally received the tragic news that her husband had died in the war. She lingered there. The letter, clasped loosely in her hand, silently dropped to the floor. Holding on to the fireplace mantle with both hands, she struggled with the emotions that swept over her like a storm driven tide. Perhaps it was the chill from the cool evening or perhaps it was because she felt colder than she ever had been, but Sally remained by the fireplace for most of the night. Every night she lit candles in memoriam to her deceased loved one and furbished a shrine on the mantel that included a lock of his hair encased in a special locket and mounted his sword on the wall above. Her grief may have iced over her emotions as well, for she never remarried. Over one hundred years later, her ghost still appears in the same place, still grieving over the news. Her ghost has been described as a tall dark-haired woman seen by the fireplace... her hands on the mantle, head slumped over, she stands weeping.

The Ferry Plantation House at dusk.

The room now serves as a conference room for craft-making and meetings and, walking in, I noticed that the room was *cold* despite Linda's efforts to insulate it. There is a recording of a conversation that, allegedly, took place between a paranormal investigator and Sally's spirit. The name "Sally" was heard. The investigator had asked her, "Why are you always standing by the fireplace?" *She* answered, "It's cold!"

Within the walls of the house lurks a child ghost or, as some refer to her, "Ferry's Little Girl" (Gilbert, Nash, Norred-Williams, 2005). She has been described as a curly-haired child, melancholy, and as if searching for something or someone and not being able to find it. She was first reported by a group of teenagers who had gained access to the house during its state of neglect. One of them happened upon the child ghost; "she" ran to the back and vanished. The group of teens understandably gave up their sense of adventure and quickly fled the house.

A minister, who was with his wife on a tour, also saw the little girl's ghost. In the dining room, he saw a little girl about the age of ten that seemed confused. She then walked through a wall. He later said, "I've seen things I should not believe in."

The Conference Room has another spirit child, this one a boy who fell out of the window. The room was formerly used as a girl's bedroom. Eric Walke was eight at the time of his death. Linda, the director of the Plantation House, is forever finding chairs grouped around a certain window...the window from which Eric had fallen. It would seem, as she surmised, that because the chairs would move by some kinetic force and gather about the same window and not any other, perhaps it is because Eric's ghost wants to keep others from the same fate by fortifying the window with chairs.

Eric has also been seen in the library.

Linda remembers one sighting of both Eric and the little girl together on the staircase. She had been carrying some items up the stairs when she saw the children. She described the girl about ten-years-old and the boy eight; they were both wearing nineteenth century period dress. What was so disconcerting was that the children had interacted with her...*by making room so that she could get by them*!

During the turn of the nineteenth century, the Barnett family owned the Ferry. Mr. Charles Barnett was a wealthy man by the time he acquired the house. While he was away, his young wife Stella had succumbed by eating a poisonous mushroom. She became very weak, but had managed to send her nine-year-old son by horseback to fetch the doctor. Unfortunately, the doctor was too late. She was dead. Stella's ghost has been seen only in the Green Room upstairs, a sitting room adjacent to the master bedroom. Temperatures drop by as much as forty degrees in the place that her body was been found, but her spirit is not a malicious one. Those who "feel" her presence tend to find comfort rather than fear.

Deadly Staircase

On the top floor are the children's bedrooms and the room where the nanny slept. Many children died at an early age due to one childhood ailment or another. In fact one family lost so many daughters that the name Margaret was given seven times! Many nannies were employed and, at times, their presence still persists. Eerie footsteps can be heard in repetitive motion...as if a nanny was going back and forth, still checking on the children. On the stairs leading up to the third floor, a caretaker had tripped on her skirts and fell down the steps, hitting her head against the wall.

During an EVP session, an investigator asked, "How did you fall down the stairs?" A woman's ghostly voice then answers, "Your children!"

Walking up these steps, I find the stairwell very narrow, and I could just imagine the ladies of the house wearing those enormous hoop skirts as they struggled up the stairs. How easy it would be to trip and fall! Linda said that at times she trips on a certain step at the top. Others say they have been slightly pushed or felt an unseen obstacle move past them as they go up or down the very same stairs.

The stairs leading to the upper floor of the Ferry Plantation House... The 2nd landing is where the nanny tumbled and hit her head. The stairs are steep!

The Parlor

Another creepy—if not downright disturbing—room of the house is the parlor. Both times upon entering it, I immediately felt an oppressive atmosphere bearing down upon me. I also felt watched. The room is darker and colder than the Conference Room. A lot of grief occurred in this room, for Linda explained that it was a room usually held for wakes and viewings. There have been reports of spectral figures clad in mourning black and soft sounds of people crying. People have reported smelling cigar smoke although smoking is prohibited. Yet the room also has an air of offensiveness other than profound sadness. There does seem to be maliciousness. Most of the visitors I spoke to report suffering from headaches as soon as they entered. Indeed, a friend of mine, Chris, who has psychic abilities, felt physically ill in the room and had to leave. She felt something getting at her. The other troubling aspect is that my recording device kept cutting off and, on play back, most of the portions in the parlor were filled with static. I also had trouble with my camera batteries, which seemed to die as soon as I replaced them. This was the only room in the house that I had trouble with my equipment. "The room has bad vibes!" aptly concludes Teddy. "Sometimes the hair on my arms stands up. I've never liked it."

Linda felt another ghostly experience when she was alone in the house. After a busy day, she took advantage of a lull between tours to do some crafting in preparation for a coming workshop. Out of the corner of her eye, she saw a shadow walk by and then she heard footsteps, loud and heavy, slowly walking about in the parlor. Each step creaked as if *he* (she sensed that it was a man) wore heavy-soled shoes, but instead of fearing an intruder, she thought he was there for a tour. However, when she checked the room, nobody was there.

The staff of volunteers (there is no paid staff, just dedicated helpers), though, aren't the only ones who have experienced ghostly sightings. While there isn't a resident cat at Ferry Plantation House, there may be a ghost cat. The cat is black with white beneath its chin; it has been sighted on occasion for the past forty-five years both in and outside the house. Some people report feeling something like a cat rubbing about their ankles and hearing meowing. Others commented on seeing a cat and holding the door open for it.

The parlor... The room in which visitors experience headaches, nausea, and batteries draining.

Old Henry

Over one hundred years ago, most of the domestic help were African American slaves. Above the old kitchen is where the slave quarters once were...and they, too, are very active with paranormal activity. EVPs of small children whimpering and footsteps were heard. One ghost was a former slave dedicated to his duties — old Henry lived in the manor house and his sole responsibility was tending the kitchen fire. Henry never left the plantation, even after he was freed, and his spirit still lingers. During the 1950s, a doctor house-sitting saw Henry doing what he used to do in his human life, tending the fire. One evening, the doctor beheld the spectral form of Henry as he walked across the room and knelt by the fireplace. He then turned and disappeared through a wall. The doctor saw the same ghost every night from then on, as Henry seemed stuck in the same routine, completely unaware of anyone around him, including the doctor. Years later, that very same wall was demolished when it was discovered that an old original staircase was behind it. The slaves' quarters were at the top of those stairs, so Henry would have to come down the stairs and cross the room to get to the fire, which makes the logistics plausible.

A Haunted Tree

The house also has a dark chapter in its history. There is a huge tree, older than the others around it, behind the house that stands as a stark reminder of the brutality of slavery. In 1802, Anthony Walke, II, hearing about a nearby slave uprising, feared the worst. He rounded up those he suspected of insurrection and ordered them, "To be hung until they rot!" Some visitors described dreams in which they saw the corpses hanging and a man weeping as he stood at the base of the tree.

I felt an overwhelming sense of sadness sweep over me. Standing in the gathering gloom, with the only illumination from porch lights of the nearby houses and flickering fireflies, I looked up at the tree. My eyes were drawn to one particular branch...a branch big and strong enough to bear a victim's full weight. I was told that most people feel that very same branch was the one used in the lynchings. My attention then turned to the base of the tree where piles of bodies once laid. Ghastly, I thought, turning away, imagining the flies and the smell.

The hanging tree... You can see the effect the
paranormal is having on my camera.

Author standing beneath the hanging tree... The expression on my face
is a reaction to the horrible history associated with the tree.

I looked back at the Ferry Plantation House that stood nearby, a testament to antebellum South. Despite the descending nightfall, its dim outlines converged into a solid presence, a decidedly looming presence. I shuddered, but eventually joined the tour as they were returning to the house. I then paused. I would have given that tree one last look over my shoulder, maybe seeing a man swaying in the breeze, a rope around his neck, but I didn't look. I didn't want to.

Despite the tragedies and grim events, the Ferry Plantation is a great place to visit for both the history buff and ghost hunter. Visitors will appreciate its wonderful architecture of a bygone era and will enjoy the lovely scenery. Perhaps you may experience a ghost or two, or perhaps not. Who is to say? But you will enjoy your visit.

~~~~~

The Old Coast Guard Life Saving Station...

Restless Spirits

During the nineteenth century, shipwrecks were common along Virginia Beach's oceanfront. From 1875 to 1915, there were more than 184 wrecks. The majority of the shipwrecks were caused by violent storms, hurricanes, and Nor'easters. These storms can generate waves up to twenty feet high and, since most Nor'easters form during the fall and winter months, they can bring snow and freezing conditions. Most of these disasters occurred because south-bound sailing vessels had to avoid the northerly Gulf Steam by hugging the coast. If bad weather struck, even experienced captains would become disoriented and inadvertently run their ships onto the beach or become lodged on a sandbar near the shore (Pouliot, 1986). The stormy sea would then take its dreadful toll, as waves would tear the hapless vessel apart, leaving its crew in danger. Some drowned in the frigid waters.

The Old Coast Guard Station... Note the resort hotel behind it.

Fortunately, the United States Life-Saving Services (USLSS) was able to rescue many. The men who manned stations along the Virginia Beach coast, including the Seatack/Virginia Beach Station, were highly trained and kept constant vigil over the seas and were quick to respond to those in peril by means of various life-saving equipment. One was a breeches buoy that transferred victims from ship to shore via a harness and pulley. As a last resort, the men would launch their life-saving boats in a rescue attempt (Chewning, 2008). These rescues were as dangerous as the shipwrecks themselves, hence the motto of the USLSS: "You have to go out, but you don't have to come back." The tragedy of such events would be evident in the aftermath, as bodies would begin to wash ashore along with the remnants of the wrecks. Identification was a painstaking process, and some, devoid of any identifying marks, were simply deemed as "Unknown." Other times appendages would wash ashore: hands, feet, legs, and arms. These parts were collected and sent to a medical examiner in hopes of identifying their origins. The survivors of these ordeals considered themselves incredibly lucky and very thankful for the USLSS's efforts.

One of the most tragic shipwrecks was the Norwegian bark, old schooner *Dictator* bound from Florida to England, carrying a cargo of timber in March 1891. Her captain, Jorgen Martinius Jorgensen, was traveling with his wife Johanne Pauline, or Paua as he affectionately called her, and his young son Carl. While it may seem unusual to sail on a commercial endeavor with one's family, Jorgensen was as dedicated to his family as he was to his ship and crew. It was an ill-fated voyage from the start. After experiencing a series of storms, the Captain decided to navigate his ship towards Virginia so that it could be repaired before attempting the transatlantic voyage. However, the seas were becoming increasingly rough as another storm began battering the already battered *Dictator*. Early morning on March 27, Good Friday, she became grounded on a sandbar 350 yards from the shore. Jorgensen might have reasoned that even though the ship might be a loss there was still time to rescue his crew.

On that fateful day, Keeper Edward Drinkwater, captain of the Seatack station who had been watching the bark as she floundered in the roiling sea, quickly dispatched his men in a rescue attempt. It was a futile one. The breeches buoy was administered first, but the pitching and rolling of the ship either caused a hapless seaman to dangle high in the air or plunge into the icy water (Foss, 1977). The ship did have a boat, but even though it made it ashore with four sailors, it had been filled with water, thus causing Drinkwater to prohibit further use. It was too great of a risk. By evening, only eight men of the crew were rescued, and the nine remaining passengers, including Johanna and the child Carl, were still aboard the rapidly deteriorating ship. Jorgensen pleaded with his frightened wife to get to shore by the breeches buoy, but she refused. In the darkness, the Captain could no longer see the shore save for a fire the Seatack crew had set. At this point, the crew knew the end was coming to the *Dictator*. In one last attempt to save his family, Jorgensen lashed a life ring to his wife and one to himself. He took his son and tied him to his chest. Bidding his dear Paua goodbye, he descended a ladder and leapt into the ravaging sea. Wave after wave washed over the brave captain, and one tore his son from him. Swimming around and around amidst flotsam, his fear became real as he searched in vain for his son, but to no avail. Carl had drowned. Johanna was swept away by a wave and drowned with the remaining crew. Jorgensen later managed to make it ashore, exhausted and in utter despair over losing his family (Ibid).

From the shore, onlookers and the men of the Seatack and Cape Henry Life Saving stations viewed this tragic event in horror. One can just imagine the weight of Drinkwater's decision and his frustration as he watched another ship and crew meet their doom. Yet to send his men out in such conditions would have been risking their own end and that was a fate he did not want his men to share.

As Virginia Beach grew into the popular resort city it is today, no one could forget the tragedy of the *Dictator*. The *Dictator* figurehead, known as the Norwegian Lady, later washed ashore and remained a fixture at the Princess Anne Hotel. It was later replaced by a statue, the New Norwegian Lady, on September 22, 1962, and stands near the Old Coast Guard Station, the former site of the Seatack/Virginia Beach Life-Saving Station. It is a sober reminder of those who perished at sea and the brave men who patrolled the coast, ready to save the unfortunate.

Stories abounded after the tragedy of the *Dictator*. The local population was saddened by the news. Particularly distressing was the news that the bodies of the crew and of Johanna had been found, but not Carl's. Then strange reports surfaced of people hearing the noise of a crying child yet never finding the source. Pitiful wailings could be heard all night, causing anxious people to wonder if there was child being neglected. Then, as mysteriously as the crying started, it abruptly stopped...just around the time that Carl's body was found and buried with his mother in a cemetery in Norfolk. Others reported seeing wraith like figures emerge out of the water and then vanish. Perhaps not the victims from the *Dictator* since there had been other tragic shipwrecks in that area, but still a terrifying sight to behold. Legend has it if you swim at the Oceanfront during the summer and feel a sudden cold spot in the water, you could be experiencing a ghostly presence (Chewning).

The Norwegian Lady Statue

This plaque commemorates all those who have been lost at sea.

The Old Coast Guard Life Saving Station was among the five Virginia Beach life-saving stations that dotted the Virginian coast. It was originally called the Seatack Life Saving Station, Station #2, and was built in 1878. Seatack is a combination of the words *sea* and *attack* that have two possible origins: the War of 1812 and the threat of the British navy and the term that meant ships sailing from Chesapeake Bay before heading east to Europe had to tack south along the coast (The Beach, 2006). It was later replaced by the Virginia Beach Life Saving Station in 1903, and then decommissioned by the United States Coast Guard in 1969. The fading years of the age of sail subsequently caused a decline for the Life Saving Service, which was later replaced by the Coast Guard. In addition, nautical devices such as radar and other communication devices replaced sea captains' penchant for "dead reckoning," making sea travel less dangerous. Today it is a museum that pays tribute to the people who braved the elements and rescued the unfortunate (Pouliot, 1986). There are over 2,000 artifacts that depict the history of the life saving service. It has two levels of interest called galleries; the first gallery depicts the history and the equipment used over the years. You will find many exhibits featuring the men and women who served. The second gallery includes an interactive exhibit of ships and ship lore, including the many shipwrecks along Virginia's coast.

It is also haunted.

Al Chewning, author of *Haunted Virginia Beach*, has a vested interest in the supernatural. Combining his love of Virginia Beach history and storytelling, he conducts "The Original Virginia Beach Ghost Walk" (more can be found at his website www.HistoriesAndHaunts.com), enthralling audiences as he describes various ghostly disturbances, which Virginia Beach has in abundance. One in particular is John Woodhouse Sparrow of the Old Coast Guard Station on 24th Street.

The men of the USLSS devoted their lives to rescuing those in dire need; one of them was Sparrow, who served for thirty years. Sparrow's photograph hangs in the museum and he represents all of the courageous men. He is standing on the beach, outfitted in a slicker and rubber boots. A lantern in his right hand and a staff in his other, his expression is stern as he peers out to sea, ever vigilant. He is also as dedicated to his duties in the afterlife as he was in life...for his spirit still keeps vigil. There have been reported sightings of a man dressed in surfman's gear and it is thought to be Sparrow. Others claim to have seen a man in the watchtower late at night. One worker at the museum was closing up shop for the day when she saw a man lingering. Looking closely, she saw that he was wearing nineteenth century apparel. When she told him that he had to leave, he did so quite literally—he vanished into thin air!

The day I dropped by the station it was a beautiful, sunny day in May. The Oceanfront was just starting to pick up steam for the coming tourist season, which typically starts Memorial Day. I took a tour of the museum and was enthralled by the history of the station. After the tour, I had a chance to speak with Julie J. Pouliot, the Administrative Director/ Museum Store Manager. Julie, along with her husband Richard, wrote *Shipwrecks on the Virginia Coast* about the plight of many sailing ships, including the *Dictator*. Straightforward but affable, she provided me a no-nonsense approach to her experiences at the museum. She always considered herself a "see it to believe it" kind of person and says, "I've always felt comfortable here, even by myself working late."

However, one day during the summer she had been in the attic, attending to the artifacts stored there, when she felt a presence. She described the usual oven-like environment of the attic on such a hot day in July, but on this particular day she felt a sudden cold draft "that came from nowhere and descended upon me." Julie had a distinct feeling of being watched as well. The attic is where the unidentified bodies and body parts were allegedly stored during the cold months before they could be properly buried.

Julie also described a woman's experience of feeling an emotional residue of great sadness attached to an ancient telephone display in the lower gallery, and as she ascended the stairs to the second floor, the stronger the feeling became until it was almost unbearable. There have been sightings of an apparition on the second floor. Chewning has in his possession a couple of pictures taken by tourists of the second-floor gallery. In one, a spectral outline of a man dressed in a slicker can be seen, and in another a spirit orb hovers in the exact location of the former. Can it be concluded that this ghostly evidence is linked to Sparrow? It has been argued that Sparrow, witnessing the decline of the services he kept, did not like the inevitable change yet remained steadfast in his duties. Perhaps he was saddened at the thought of no longer being needed and carried this feeling after his death.

Sparrow, ever the devoted surfman, still watches over the coastline... even in the afterlife.

~~~~~

Other Virginia Beach Haunts

The Cavalier Hotel

In April 1926, the Cavalier made its debut as one of the Atlantic Seaboard's most famous hotels. The hotel was renowned for its splendor and sophistication and famous guests. Among the many who have stayed in its luxurious rooms were screen legends Louise Brooks, Judy Garland, Bette Davis, and Betty Grable. Also in the guest book were former presidents Herbert Hoover, Dwight Eisenhower, John F. Kennedy, and Richard Nixon. It also has its share of ghosts.

Guests have reported odd occurrences including pounding on the walls during the middle of the night, which prompted calls to the front desk that yield little to no explanation upon investigation. One guest heard voices coming from the bathroom only to find no one there. Others claim feeling "watched" in the lobby. Ghostly figures of an elderly woman clad in antiquated fur stole and hat walking her dog on the front lawn and an African American male servant that walks through the walls have been reported.

In 1927, Coors icon Adolph Coors leapt to his death in an alleged suicide — some say he was pushed — from the sixth floor. Some claim to have witnessed his apparition walking the halls dressed elegantly in tux and tails. The sixth floor also contains another ghost: a gentleman clad in the hotel's old staff uniform. Upon research no one can verify any staff member that fits his description working at the hotel within the past decade. Others report seeing a tabby cat roaming about on the grounds and in the halls, but when getting close enough to pet it, see it vanish. Through the years, managers and employees can neither confirm nor deny these paranormal occurrences.

Adam Thoroughgood House

Originally from Norfolk, England, Adam Thoroughgood was a rags-to-riches story. He came to Virginia in 1621 as an indentured servant, working until he was granted his freedom in 1624. He then returned to England to marry Sarah Offley, daughter of a wealthy merchant. When he settled in the Lynnhaven area, he was wealthy enough to purchase 5,350 acres of land. Adam Thoroughgood's (Thorowgood) grandson built the house in 1680. Many owners have resided in the house throughout the years, thus establishing it as a historic site in 1971, but the hauntings have been around much longer. Former owners reported seeing gradual indentations of a person's head on a pillow in the upstairs bedroom mysteriously appear and disappear. A former employee saw two ghostly women dressed in period costume sitting on the chairs in the kitchen, only to slowly fade away. Visitors have witnessed a flicker of a shadow ascending the stairs, and one person claimed to experience a person standing close enough to have the hairs on her arm bristle although no one was near.

A House in Laurel Cove

Strange occurrences at this house have led many to believe that it is caused by poltergeist activity. The neighborhood was developed in the late 1960s. The land was originally a dairy farm owned by the Conrad family, and before the farm, stood many residences, some dating back to the eighteenth century. One house in particular was built on an ancient Native American burial ground and is located across from a graveyard. A family who settled into the house was soon experiencing the unexplained: footfall, doors opening and closing, and disembodied voices.

The haunting didn't end with strange sounds, though. Soon the family witnessed furniture moving before their eyes. A framed picture crashed to the floor. Dinner became frightening as plates of food were flung about and cups and glasses moved on their own. Even more disconcerting was a child's handprint smeared on mirrors, surfaces, and windows.

The haunting seemed to be a "family" of ghosts, for they heard a woman's voice and saw an apparition of what appeared to be a man in the living room. The family eventually learned that the ghosts haunting their house were indeed a family: George Williamson, his wife, and daughter who perished there in a house fire. As with any other haunted house, the family learned to live with their otherworldly housemates (Gilbert, Lillie, Nash, & Norred-Williams, 2005).

False Cape

A child's cries are heard in the evenings when the still of the day occurs. The crying is described as pitiful. Any parent or caretaker is almost tormented by the hapless wails. No child has been found in the area as a victim or otherwise, and nobody knows what causes the child to cry.

Chesapeake

The city of Chesapeake is relatively new to Hampton Roads: Norfolk County and the city of South Norfolk merged in 1963, creating Chesapeake. The city always had its rural charm with the development of familiar landmarks such as Pleasant Grove, Great Bridge, Oak Grove, Fentress, South Norfolk, Portlock, Deep Creek, Western Branch, Indian River, and Hickory occurring in the early 1900s. With residential and commercial development, Chesapeake grew from a "community crossroads" (Harper, 2008).

~~~~~

The Haunted Locales...

Bruce-Speers House

According to *A History of Chesapeake, Virginia* by Raymond L. Harper, this house has a history of strange goings on. Built over three hundred years ago, the house has weathered the various changes, including the Civil War. Mrs. Louisa Bruce King was a staunch supporter of the Confederate Army. When a Yankee soldier threatened her homestead, she was no wilting southern belle. She grabbed a rifle and shot the man, burying him under the house. To this day, the soldier's ghost still haunts the house.

The Ghost Child of Great Bridge

The story describes a child who got lost during the construction of the municipal buildings. The child had wandered over to the site and was killed. To this day you can see the child's frail spirit, small footprints, and if you listen very hard you can hear his soft cries.

Chapter Three:

Portsmouth

Oftentimes in the shadow of Williamsburg and Norfolk in terms of popular historic sites, Portsmouth's roots run deeper in the Hampton Roads area than the rest of the cities combined. In 1608, the legendary Captain John Smith, famous for his descriptions of the New World, sailed down the Elizabeth River and happened to come upon an abandoned Indian village. From this ancient site sprang a new civilization as the city of Portsmouth grew from a seaside port to the city it is now. From the early populations of the seventeenth century, the Revolutionary War, and the Civil War, Portsmouth's Naval shipyard played a significant role in shipbuilding and repair, which could explain its haunted reputation.

~~~~~

Trinity Episcopal Church

Formally known as Portsmouth Parish of the Church of England, Trinity Church was built in 1762 and thus began a history of devout worship and service to the faithful. In 1774, Reverend John Braidfoot became the second rector. The Scotsman joined the Revolutionary War as a chaplain. He served until the war ended, and then returned to his church where he later ministered until his death in 1786.

The details of his death are mysterious. One frosty night on February 6, 1785, Braidfoot was making his way home after a long journey. He was on horseback and the trip had been tiring. Suddenly, his horse reared, almost knocking him off. Trying to calm his horse, Braidfoot beheld a frightening sight: a wraith that prophesied his doom. The figure was a floating woman clad in diaphanous gown, and he could see the shrubbery behind her. Her eyes were livid in her pale face as she

Trinity Episcopal Church

The graveyard of Trinity Episcopal Church

coldly stared down at him. In voice that chilled him to his bones, she said, "Braidfoot! Hear me now! Ye have only a year to live. Make your amends and say your goodbyes, for on the night a year from now, ye shall die!" She disappeared, but her words still echoed in the chilly night, turning his heart into ice. Finally in the safety of his house, he related the tale to his sympathetic wife. He could not sleep that night as he still could see that hideous face and those penetrating eyes, not to mention the terrible doom that had befallen him. In the days after, the memory of that terrible night slowly receded as his service to the church allowed him to take solace in his faith. Perhaps, he reasoned it was a dream. He was exhausted that night.

Exactly a year after that event, the terrible memory bubbled up like rotten fish. Was he actually to die February 6, 1786? Would it come true? His wife, seeing his distressed state, offered to cheer him up by planning a lavish dinner and inviting some friends for a pleasant evening. Braidfoot was distracted, but relented to please his wife. The dinner was a success: the food delicious and the company jovial. Braidfoot did enjoy himself as he engaged in such delights. However, as the night continued, he felt something tugging at his conscious. He abruptly excused himself and retired to his bedchamber. Concerned, his wife soon followed. The guests were startled by her screams, and rushed into the room. There they found Braidfoot...dead. The look on his face was of sheer fear. There were no signs of foul play, as Braidfoot was literally frightened to death.

Some say the spirit of Braidfoot haunts the graveyard of Trinity Church. Witnesses say that his ghost walks from one end of the cemetery to the other and vanishes. A police car following what appeared to be a dark shape stopped by the Church. When the policeman got out to investigate, he saw the shape entering the church. He could not find it whatever it was. Perhaps it is the ghost of Braidfoot?

Portsmouth Naval Medical Center

Along the Elizabeth River in downtown Portsmouth, Virginia, stands the Portsmouth Naval Medical Hospital. The hospital was built from the remains of a fort, Fort Nelson, long abandoned, and the first building was finished in 1830. Since the early nineteenth century, Building Number One, its foundation laid in 1827, has treated the nation's military through several epidemics and many wars (Garrigues, 1998). In the early nineteenth century, the design of the hospital was to accommodate up to five hundred patients. Occasionally there were forty patients at a given time. During the summer of 1855, the hospital received a flood of patients during the Yellow Fever epidemic: 587 civilian patients were admitted over the next few months; 208 died and 379 recovered and were eventually discharged (Ibid). If the casualties of pestilence tested the doctors' mettle, the Civil War proved hospital worthy of historical significance.

During the Civil War, the battlefield scene was tragic to behold: young men being shot, bludgeoned, stabbed by bayonets, or blown apart by cannon fire. The wounded were brought to field hospitals. The mere utterance of the surgeon's diagnosis "amputation" instilled fear in even the most battle-hardened soldier. Horrible accounts of body parts piled high outside field hospitals, stacked to the height of a standing man, surgeons' clothes and forearms smeared with gore, and the screams of men unfortunate not to have an anesthetic probably had given this practice a bad reputation. Amputations during the Civil War were routine. Surgeons used handsaws to sever appendages, and no ranking official was immune to this practice as generals as well as privates underwent such treatment. Amputations could be done quickly if the surgeon was skilled enough and most surgeons felt they were necessary in order to save lives. However, most soldiers died because of infection brought on by amputation than on the battlefield.

The Civil War was the bloodiest conflict in American history. Up to four million Union and Confederate soldiers fought in the Civil War. Of this number, 184,594 were killed in combat, but 373,458 died from infection and disease (Holcomb, 1930). Neither side was prepared for the decimation on the male population that would last for four long years (Uschan, 2005). Particularly affected was the medical field. The practice of medicine in the nineteenth century was in denial over the theory that most illness was caused by bacteria. Long before modern medical practice such as antiseptics and sterilization became the norm, men died of infections caused by dirty instruments and the lack of hand-washing. Injury from a bullet or cannonball caused considerably less damage than disease. From the battlefield, to field hospital, to military hospitals, the cruel irony of medical personnel regarding surgeons' ignorance about disease is that most infected and killed the very lives they were responsible for saving (Ibid). W. W. Keen, a Union surgeon, describes his experience:

> We operated on old blood–stained and often pus-stained coats, the veterans of a hundred fights…if a sponge fell or an instrument fell on the floor it was washed and squeezed in a basin of tap water and used as if it were clean. (Uschan, 2005)

In early 1865, Ensign Robley D. Evans was wounded at Fort Fisher and brought to the Norfolk Naval Hospital, as it was then called. He was eighteen and his legs had suffered a serious injury, and the surgeons hastily advised amputation. In an interview years later, Evans, proud in his stubbornness, argues, "I preferred to die with my legs on," and turned his gun on his doctors. "I would kill six before they cut my legs off" (Holcomb, 1930). Although gravely injured, he fought to keep his legs and won, but he suffered the disgusting conditions of the hospital including cockroaches, rats, and mice that took up residence: "No language of man can convey any idea of the quantity and variety of vermin in that hospital" (Ibid). He later developed erysipelas (a bacterial skin disease indicated by a severe rash) caused by an attendant who used a dirty sponge, which was later followed by an abscess in his knee. Evans survived his ordeal and later became captain of the *Iowa* in the Spanish-American War. Most weren't so lucky.

Civil War military hospitals tended to be as filthy as field hospitals despite the dedicated team of medical personnel. Men who suffered the horrors of amputations, but were given a good prognosis fell victim to hospital gangrene, septicemia, erysipelas, tetanus, or a host of maladies brought on by the various insects that feasted on their injured flesh because of unscreened windows. Many suffered terribly from fevers and pain before they succumbed. One such man died a miserable death due to an infection brought on by amputation, and his ghost remains an eternal witness to the horrors of the Civil War.

In the early years of the war, between 1861 and 1862, Confederate forces occupied the hospital. A man was admitted to the hospital suffering from a serious leg wound. He was barely conscious, so he was unaware of the prognosis: amputation. Thankfully, he was given anesthesia as his leg was sawed off. As he woke in the gray dawn to the radiating pain from his missing leg, he agonized over the sight of his weeping stump. His future looked grim: how was he to work with one leg and provide for a family? He gazed around him at the other patients lying on cots that lined the stained concrete walls. He saw one man whose head was completely bandaged to the extent that only one eye was revealed. The man gazed dully at him with his one good eye. Other men lay prone with their appendages bandaged or, like his, missing. He saw men bemoaning their pain: men who wept with shame and fear, or men whose faces resembled statues, sitting staring into nothing. Attending to these were several female nurses. Most of these nurses were seasoned in such calamities and gave what little consolation to their pain before moving on to the next patient. One caught his eye. She was young, maybe early twenties, and her face beheld the innocence of a child, as if bereft of the surrounding suffering and the brutalities of war. She was fair and strands of blonde hair that was covered by the standard bonnet loosened and fell about her face. One she took and smoothed behind her bonnet. She looked weary though very pretty as she sat by one wounded man, reading a letter from his family. He stared at her until she looked up at him. The best medicine she gave him was a radiant smile.

The next few days, he watched her as she came and went, attending to patients' needs, assisting the surgeons on their rounds, or consoling the men with letters, reading the Bible, or simply holding a hand and offering comfort. He was eventually fitted with a peg leg that he could hardly use since his leg was still traumatized by the amputation, but the doctors were insistent and had him walk about with it. He gritted his teeth and endured the pain. His will was strong, particularly when he glimpsed his beloved nurse. However, before he could learn her name, his wound became hot and hotter still. The bandages oozed yellow from pus. Maggots wriggled in the gangrene-infected meat of his stump. "Where is my leg?" he yelled at the doctors. "Give me back my leg!" For many days thereafter, he writhed in the heat of a fever, screaming at the dream phantoms his dying brain induced. He slipped in and out of conscious. He once woke briefly to the sensation of coolness on his forehead. It was the nurse's cool hand. She smiled down at him. He smiled back before closing his eyes forever.

The Ghost of Building 1, as it is called, roams parts of the hospital. I spoke to Al Cutchin, a former Portsmouth Naval Medical Center (as it is now called) employee and historian, about the ghost. Until renovations were done in 2002, the ghost was seen in and around Building 1. During the 1960s, he told me, some of the medical staff sprinkled talcum powder on the top floor in hopes of gaining some evidence of the rumored ghost. As they waited, they heard thumping and dragging noises as if someone was limping heavily. They looked but nothing was there, but when they checked the powder they found the tell-tale tracks of a man with one leg: a footprint and a small dent in the sand—the peg leg. Frightened, they gazed at one another and realized it was a ghost that they heard. As if on cue, they then heard the noises of someone in pain. The sounds of agonizing shrieks that ended in moans, grunting, and someone yelling resonated along the floor. The more daring of the staff wanted to stay and communicate with it, but the ones with greater common sense quickly departed the scene. Others say that the same sounds could be heard in what is known as the "dungeon." More likely it was used as storage space during the war than an actual detainment facility. On the fifth floor, which is the top floor, used to be an operating room and a morgue.

Needless to say that Portsmouth Naval Medical Center has attained an outstanding reputation of a professional and well-equipped hospital staffed with capable surgeons, specialists, nurses, and other medical personnel who are well educated and prepared for most cases that enter. But the eerily echoing sounds still reverberate in its halls. Perhaps it is that Confederate soldier searching for his leg?

The Olde Towne District

One gorgeous but cool spring day, I had the wonderful opportunity to take a private tour of the homes and churches in the Olde Towne Historic District, courtesy of Portsmouth historian Dean Burgess. A man who had boundless energy despite his age, Mr. Burgess guided me through three hundred years of history as he pointed out various houses and the famous persons who had once resided there as well as their historical influence. After the tour, our journey ended back at his house and we parted ways. For all throughout the two-hour tour, while my feet ached for a hot soak, his enthusiasm remained high. Mr. Burgess is a truly dedicated man in maintaining Portsmouth's heritage. There are ghosts. Although he did not tell me any ghost stories, he did explain how the area played a major role in not only shaping Portsmouth as an important city in Hampton Roads, but as a crucial part of American history. Wandering around the neighborhood is similar to stepping back in time despite the modern automobiles parked along the street and satellite dishes mounted to roofs. The district has many beautiful homes that vary in architectural styles that include Victorian, Georgian, Classical Renaissance, Gothic, and Romanesque. Most of these homes are private residences...and a few are said to be haunted.

The Grice-Neely House

The house dates back to 1820 and resembles houses found in New Orleans with its wrought iron balconies that frame the front of the house. Over a hundred years ago, the domestic help was often housed in small dwellings behind the main home. One of them was Isaiah and his family.

One balmy evening, Isaiah took his son fishing along the Elizabeth River. Conversation was light, for they only spoke about the details of the sport and little else, but it was a good time for Isaiah since he rarely had the chance to be with him. Beneath the full moon, father and son caught enough fish to last them for a few days. The tide was turning and the current became stronger, so they decided to head home. Yet the lighthearted fun gave way to tragedy as his son slipped on the pilings and fell into the churning waters. The father called for help and scanned the river's dark surface for any sign of his son. Finally, he couldn't wait any longer and jumped in the water. After rescuing his son and pulling him to shore, Isaiah lost his footing and fell backwards into the river. The current was too strong and pulled him under. Those who gathered to help never saw him break the surface, and his body was never found.

His spirit lingers at the Grice-Neely House.

Years later, a tenant awoke one night to find a shadow at the foot of her bed. She tried to scream, but the shape stood there, not moving towards her. The full moon drifted in and out of the clouds, and finally it flooded her bedroom with its light, so she managed to see his face. He was African American, tall, and dressed in clothes of the last century. Something in his features touched her; he seemed so sad. He gazed at her, or rather through her, and then as the moon slid behind a cloud and the room again plunged into darkness, he disappeared. Needless to say, sleep was not forthcoming to her at all that night.

Others have seen his ghost in the garden where the dependency once stood. His expression is always the same—sad—but some have said that he appears to be searching for something or someone. Perhaps Isaiah is still searching for his son after all these years (Leitner, 1991).

The Grice-Neely House

The Gaffos House

It was July 1855 and the height of the Yellow Fever epidemic was under way. A man staggers out of a house used as a temporary hospital. The lines etched on his face were from grief and lack of sleep. He had just lost his daughter from the ravages of the fever during the previous night. The hospital was overflowing with the sick and the dying and could do little to comfort him over his loss. Overwhelmed, he struggled outside for fresh air, but the smells that emanated from the empty streets were of camphor and decaying bodies, making him wretch. He then wiped his mouth and saw the death mark—a smear of black vomit. Wracked with bone breaking pain and fever induced chills, he knew he was a doomed man. Yet his heart found solace at the thought of reuniting with his daughter.

The Gaffos House stands as a testament to the Yellow Fever epidemic that raged through the summer of 1855. It served as one of the many makeshift hospitals during the pestilence. How many people perished in the house is unknown, for many victims couldn't or weren't identified, just nameless casualties of the disease. The pestilence started with something as small as a mosquito. In June 1855, the steamer *Ben Franklin* arrived from St. Thomas in the Danish West Indies. Reports from that area included cases of the Yellow Fever. By the time the ship reached Portsmouth, two men had succumbed to the disease, so it was quarantined. By then, the crew had deserted her. Before they did, however, they had pumped the bilge water that was infested with mosquito larvae into the river, which thus caused the epidemic (Forrest, 1856).

During that long, hot summer, citizens, neighbors, and families fell in the wake of Yellow Fever. Carts piled high with bodies echoed in the empty streets as drivers delivered victims to be buried. Some were turned away due to lack of room! By August, the city was deserted. One gentleman laments, "Poor Portsmouth! She presents a sad and desolate appearance" (Ibid) ... for those who remained found shelter and care among the sick and dying. In fact, any available house was used for temporary hospitals or orphanages since the majority of families were decimated, leaving a small population of parentless children. Fortunately, as the weather cooled, the tropical virus could not survive and the epidemic waned. Before it did, Portsmouth's population had been reduced significantly — ten percent of the population died from it and the rest fled the city.

The Gaffos House

Until recently, the Gaffos house was renovated from an apartment building during the war years to the grand four-story house it is now. A family excitedly moved in and took delight in its English-style basement and history. What they didn't anticipate, however, was the house being haunted.

The eerie goings on began with the strange sounds of heavy footsteps ascending the stairs to the top floor, walking about, and then coming back down the staircase. The children heard it first. The parents were at first bemused by such a tale and dismissed it as active imaginations. However, when the mistress of the house heard the very same footfall, she knew the company she kept within the house was not of this world. As the years passed, the ghostly sounds increased and even began to affect the dog.

Once, alone in the house, the mother heard strange noises coming from the living room. She then noticed the dog as she stood by the second-floor landing and growled...all of her attention focused on the living room below. Then suddenly, the dog scrambled down the stairs. Baffled, the woman could do nothing but follow. She entered the living room to find her dog engaged in a ferocious attack to what she perceived as thin air. It was something the dog could only sense and the attack was increasingly becoming more vicious as the dog would lunge snarling and growling and then quickly scamper back, whining. This happened again and again, until quite suddenly, the dog fled out of the room, through the back, and smashed through a screened door in her attempt to flee whatever was chasing her. To this day, whenever the dog is near the living room, she growls (Leitner, 1991).

What could be haunting the Gaffos House? Witnesses claim to have seen the shadowy figure of a man in front of the house. Most hesitate to call the police about an intruder because the ghost enters the front door by going through it. Others describe seeing the same ghost wearing tattered nineteenth century attire and gaunt as if diseased. Could it be that nameless victim whose daughter had perished and later died? Perhaps the heavy footfalls indicate that he is searching for his daughter and is unable to locate her. Later, after it was discovered that the Gaffos House was used as a temporary hospital and the details fell into place, the family who own the house feel less afraid and are more sympathetic of the ghost's pitiful plight. Now all they can do is learn to live with it.

Olde Towne's Other Haunted Houses

The Constant Gardener at Glencoe Inn

Witnesses describe the ghost as a woman in her eighties and dressed in nineteenth century period dress. A very benign ghost, she is thought to be a former resident who simply loved her garden so much that she is loath to leave it!

Maupin House's Mystery Lady

A ghost named Edmonia haunts this home. She's been seen descending the staircase and setting off the alarm. One night, the alarm had tripped, resulting in the local fire department responding. When they arrived, no one was home and there was no fire. Others claim to have seen her wandering among the trees in the backyard. She is a mystery for no one is quite sure how she came to be.

Oh Captain! My Captain...
The Maxwell House

A sea captain originally built the house...and his ghost remains a fixture. The ghostly presence of this captain first involved mysterious cigar smoke. This was indeed very strange to smell tobacco smoke when no one around...until Richard Maxwell, who owned the house for over twenty years, came upon the ghost sitting in a chair smoking a pipe. That would explain the odor! (Leitner, 1991) Prior to the Maxwells, over three generations of the Bunn family had resided in this house and they also witnessed this strange apparition and more. Two men, usually dressed in seafaring uniforms, have materialized before various members of the family. No sounds emit when beholding the spirits.

Chapter Four:
Suffolk

Known as Surprising Suffolk, this city on the outer edges of Hampton Roads lives up to its adage.

~~~~~

The Prentis House

Nestled in the heart of downtown Suffolk, the Prentis House has withstood the test of time. Located on North Main Street, the three-story house was built around 1800. Peter Bowdoin Prentis purchased the house in 1857, living there until his death in 1889. Peter Prentis came from a distinguished family that was most prominent in politics of the time. Joseph Prentis, his grandfather, was a judge, member of the Virginia Convention in 1775, member of the House of Delegates in 1777-78, Speaker of the House, and Judge of the General Court of Virginia from 1788 to 1809 (Woodard, 2000). His father, Joseph Prentis, II, served as a Clerk of the Nansemond County Court for thirteen years up until his death in 1851. Peter Prentis, following in his grandfather and father's footsteps, was a judge for two years and later a Clerk of the County for thirty years. He and his wife had only one child, Martha.

During the Civil War, when Suffolk was under Union occupation, Peter Prentis was held hostage at Fort Monroe and then later at Fort Norfolk. He was later released and returned to Suffolk and began to reconstruct town.

Many owners have lived in the house since the remaining descendents of the Prentis family sold it. The house was later made into an apartment building, which subsequently fell into neglect and decay. For over three decades the house stood as an eyesore for many who traveled along busy North Main Street. From the peeling paint, boarded up windows, to the weed choked front lawn, the house did indeed look spooky enough to be considered haunted, but the only activity that emanated from it was illegal, as squatters took temporary shelter in it and partying teenagers used it for illicit purposes. In 2002, after the house was renovated, it was made the base of operations for the Suffolk Visitor's Center. Today the house is open to the public, and even though the furnishings are not the original pieces, the house still retains its original structure and floorboards. The main floor resembles the room layout of the original house, the basement serves as a gift shop/reception room, and the upper floors serves as offices.

And...it is reportedly haunted.

The Prentis House

The eerie goings on at the Prentis House has baffled many. Former residents who lived there when it was an apartment building claimed to hear ghostly footsteps echoing loudly at night, feeling cold spots in the halls, and other strange happenings. The occurrences continued even after the house was refurbished into a visitor's center. According to a newspaper article in *The Virginian-Pilot*, employees would find appliances turning on and off by themselves, sounds of footfall pounding up and down the staircase, and doors opening and then slamming shut on their own accord. A cleaning crew that had arrived one morning to begin readying the center for the day discovered that all the faucets in the bathrooms were streaming water. The taps had apparently been left on all night long (Speidell, 2003). Another time a witness saw a remote control rise and then crash into a nearby wall. Could this be the spirit of Peter Prentis? The employees feel that the ghost is an added incentive for working there, finding the whole notion of a supernatural element exciting. One employee, Angela, has been quoted as saying, "A ghost actually makes working here a little more adventurous" (Speidell, 2003).

The Lakeland Skeptics Society

What haunts the Prentis House has also drawn interest from those who investigate paranormal activity. The Lakeland Skeptics Society is a local paranormal club comprised of high school students from Lakeland High in Suffolk. Marcus Daniels, who teaches earth science and oceanography at the school, leads the team. One afternoon after school, I had a chance to speak with Mr. Daniels and some members of the team: Virginia D., Danielle H., Thomas H., and Kayla S. I arrived very late since I followed the rather convoluted directions from an online directions/locator service, so I was anticipating a rushed interview and disgruntled interviewees who had to wait for so long. Instead, Mr. Daniels and his students were very gracious and accommodating as they explained their team's mission. They use the scientific method, which begins by forming a hypothesis and conducting experiments to investigate claims of the supernatural. They are, hence the name, skeptic until they rule out every cause before reaching a conclusion. Typically, Mr. Daniels argues, an old house will have creaks and groans that might *seem* spooky, but to automatically associate those creaks and groans with ghosts would be conjecture.

Indeed, most legitimate paranormal investigators worth their salt rely on ordinary logic rather than assumption. Danielle explains that the environment (i.e., extraneous noises and interference) is usually the cause rather than a suspected ghost.

Mr. Daniels adds, "If we can't come up with an explanation, that still doesn't mean it is a haunting. But it is something that is happening out of the ordinary. It's happening out of our sensory perception because obviously it is something that we do not have the understanding of."

The team spent seven hours at the Prentis House, which yielded some rather interesting results. They found evidence of both an intelligent and residual haunting. Various EVPs gave the team evidence of an intelligent entity. When an investigator asked if the spirit could make the room cold, the voice answers, "no." The team filmed a hovering orb of light near the staircase that they could not verify with their instruments. The residual evidence included the sounds of doors opening and closing and knocking, but no apparition sightings. Because they could not verify what they had experienced, the team then concluded, based on a vote, that the Prentis house is haunted.

Perhaps there is something that we do not understand that exists within the Prentis House, or maybe the presence doesn't understand the state of its existence. We share the same dilemma, don't we? Our perception of the world is far more complex than we can explain and the way we understand things is vastly influenced by our reality. Mr. Daniels points to the evidence, saying, "Evidence can only influence your own personal beliefs." We strive to discover what we can't understand by using various methods to reach a conclusion, only to ask more questions. Perhaps the spirit is experiencing the same.

~~~~~

Riddick's Folly House

I found this house to have a rather unique name as well as history. The man who inspired its creation was Mills Riddick (1780-1844). He was the son of a significant family in Suffolk and Nansemond counties and the grandson of Col. Willis S. Riddick, a hero of the Revolutionary War and a captain of cavalry during the War of 1812. In 1829, Mills Riddick served as a member of the Virginia House of Delegates, representing

Suffolk and Nansemond counties. He was also a very prosperous plantation owner and businessman of a successful lumber company. When a fire
destroyed several of his properties in 1837, he used the insurance money
to build a twelve-bedroom house in which he could live out his golden
years (Riddick's Folly, 2009). The "folly" was the incongruity of style: a
Greek Revival in the midst of the standard architectural design.

Riddick's Folly House

After his death in 1844, his widow, Mary Taylor Riddick, chose not to
live in the home. The home was then passed on to their son, Nathaniel,
and his wife and their children. A year before the Civil War broke out,
Nathaniel left the house and relocated to Petersburg, Virginia. When they

returned, they found their home in disarray. The Union had occupied the house in their absence. The violation of their home was evident: broken and missing furniture, smashed crockery, trash lay strewn about, and even some of the ladies' dresses had been worn during fits of a few soldiers' drunken debauchery, leaving them torn and stained. Some of the women's sewing baskets were all that remained intact.

The house was eventually left to the remaining Riddick descendents; one of them, Anna Mary, lived in the house until her death in 1936 at the age of 95. Friends and relatives described her as a feisty little redheaded child and later a strong-willed woman who was the first woman to vote in her time. She apparently had a passion for sewing, as her photograph depicts, most certainly out of necessity, but perhaps for relaxation, too. She is thought to be the first baby born at Riddick's Folly House and the last remaining descendent to die there.

She is also believed to be still residing there...*as a ghost.*

Most of the haunting consists of the sounds of footfalls and experiencing unexplained power outages. A former employee described an experience where a sewing basket of needlework rose off the bed and fell to the floor. While this was disconcerting enough, all the lights then went out. Perhaps it was Anna, upset that her sewing basket was put in the wrong place and wanted the staff to know not to do it again!

~~~~~

Cedar Hill Cemetery

What better place is there than a cemetery to see a ghost?

Off North Main Street across from the Prentis House is Cedar Hill Cemetery. The cemetery is thirty-seven acres of lush fields and rolling terrain containing some of the city's most prominent deceased residents. The gravestones are of particular appeal: looming obelisks in honor of fallen soldiers of the Civil War, Victorian statues of angels and other charming figurines, and some ancient gravestones dating back almost two hundred years...so old that the etchings of the markers have faded over the years.

Originally constructed as Green Hill Cemetery, the city has owned it since 1802 (Speidell, 2007). Many of the citizens of Suffolk can trace much of their lineage to those buried there, and the historical significance of the place resonates with famous figures such as former Virginia Governor Mills E. Godwin, Jr. and Edward Everett Holland, former Suffolk mayor, state senator, and U.S. Congressman. The Civil War also contributed to the deaths of both Union and Confederate soldiers, yet most of the soldiers' graves are unmarked. In 1999, the descendents of an African-American Confederate soldier, Jason Boon, who is buried there, were honored in a ceremony that marked his and other African-American soldiers' involvement in the Civil War (McNatt, 1999). Native Americans, slaves, and freed African-Americans are buried in the cemetery, too.

Cedar Hill Cemetery

Sue Woodard serves as executive director of the Suffolk-Nansemond Historical Society and is truly dedicated to her work. She conducts lantern tours at the cemetery to honor Suffolk's rich history. A courteous and hospitable woman, she described to me an experience that she finds difficult to explain. In 1997, a dedication for two restored monuments to local Confederate soldiers by the Sons of Confederate Veterans took place in the cemetery and was being videotaped for prosperity's sake. When the film was later viewed, the presence of a shadowing figure hovering about the gravestones befuddled many. The figure was a young man dressed in a uniform and appeared completely oblivious to those around him. While the uniform wasn't so unusual since those attending the ceremony were in period costume, no one could rightfully identify the youth, for none could even recall seeing him at the event. What was even more disturbing is that the videotape was later transferred into DVD format and, during the process, the image had disappeared. Everything else remained *except* for that image. Mrs. Woodard commented that the man was seen near the Phillips grave marker. Perhaps the youth was trying to join his family? No one knows for sure.

It was very quiet the day I visited the cemetery and, by the shady areas, I can see why the living seek respite among the dead in such a place. The serenity of the place soothed me as I walked among the stones, being careful not to step on any graves. Among them I located the Prentis family plot. I was struck by the gravestones of children, who unfortunately perished frequently in those days. Small stone lambs, cherubs, and other divine statues marked their final resting places. Saddened, I continued my solitary walk. I didn't experience anything unusual that day, but I did have a chance to actually visit the people who contributed to Suffolk's history. And for this I am most grateful.

Chapter Five:

The Great Dismal Swamp

> 'Tis a wild spot, and even in summer hours,
> With wondrous wealth of beauty and
> a charm
> For the sad fancy, hath the gloomiest look,
> That awes with strange repulsion.
>
> — William Gilmore Simms,
> "The Edge of the Swamp"

The Great Dismal Swamp is located between Suffolk and Chesapeake, extending below the Virginia/North Carolina border. It is 111,203 acres of wetlands and forest, but despite its dreary moniker, it is a serene and undisturbed place. At its heart is Lake Drummond, named after Lord Drummond, the first governor of North Carolina, who proposed to drain and farm it, which began a long procession of failed attempts to tame the wildness of the Swamp. The Swamp retains historical significance as well. George Washington surveyed the Swamp in 1763 and later camped by the shores of Lake Drummond. It is a place of enigmatic loveliness that has inspired poets such as H. W. Longfellow and Thomas Moore, and its sublime beauty allegedly moved Edgar Allan Poe to write his famous poem of lamentation and regret, "The Raven," while staying at the now defunct Lake Drummond Hotel, also known as the Halfway House (named as such because it had spanned the border of Virginia and North Carolina).

The Swamp gets its rather gloomy name from the early English settlers, who originally called it "the Desert" because of the harsh and unpleasant landscape that seemed unfit for citizens "seeking more genial natures" (Gilbert and Shufer, 2004). Yet the Swamp is home to many, not just wildlife. It has gone from small camps of boaters, shinglers, fishermen, and laborers to homesteaders and farmers, which resulted in a thriving "swamp community" that still exists today. It has been described as a world within a world.

The swamp is a bad place according to most locals, despite it being a national park and wildlife refuge and renowned for its vivid array of fauna, flora, and wild birds. Stories of ghosts, witches, and even a half man/half bear creature similar to Bigfoot have added to the mysterious allure of the Swamp. One of the Native American legends describes its origins by a fiery bird that raked the earth with its huge claws, causing a huge basin that filled with water. Part of what makes the Dismal Swamp such a fearsome place is how it concealed fugitives and criminals. Bootleggers had set up their illegal distillers and at times defended them with violence. There were blood-chilling tales of bandits, cutthroats, and thieves who preyed on the unwary traveler. These ruthless criminals showed no mercy and sent chills down the collective spine of the swamp community.

Yet some found the darkness and dankness a perfect cover. Henry W. Longfellow and Harriet Beecher Stowe wrote about how the Swamp was both a refuge and a dangerous place. Speculation of the number of runaways varies, but over 1,000 runaway slaves found the Swamp as a sanctuary. It is the very reputation of the Swamp being an inhospitable place that drew runaway slaves, perhaps knowing that no one would brave the elements by following them. The nineteenth century romantic writer and explorer of the Swamp, Porte Crayon, illustrated one runaway slave who found refuge in the Swamp. He is depicted as climbing out of the dense underbrush clutching a rifle. A fearsome person for any to behold, especially in the middle of the night, but no matter how formidable his expression is, he was probably scared and hungry, barely eking out an existence in such a wretched place. Men, women, and children found the Swamp's wilderness as shelter, and some men found work hauling and loading shingles, a lucrative, no-questions-asked business at the time, by blending in with freed slaves and hired hands. Some slaves created communities called the Maroon Colonies (Gilbert and Shufer, 2004). However, others succumbed to the miserable conditions of hunger, filth, disease, poisonous snakes, biting insects, and the ever-present danger of slave hunters. In 1861, Frederick Law Olmsted wrote, "Children were born, bred, lived, and died here" (Bland, 1990). Skeletal remains of these children and others depict their hardship and misery, and most were victims of the often cruel practice of slave hunters to capture slaves using dogs, guns, and traps. But most freedom seekers would rather have been shot or swallowed up whole by the Swamp than be captured. The runaway slave legacy was part of the antebellum passageway to the North known as the Underground Railroad. For more information or to view this historic place, go to www.greatdismalswamp@fws.gov.

Today visitors to the Swamp would stand in the presence of these former freedom seekers. For those sensitive enough to feel the echoes of their suffering, an overwhelming emotional response has been reported, as visitors experiencing sudden crying spells and other sorrowful reactions is common. One woman was near the remains of Dismal Town with her party when she suddenly felt dizzy. Wave after wave of inexplicable grief swept over her. Not wanting to tell the others, she hung back behind the group. As she caught her breath, she could hear faint calls of children, moans, and cries of anguish. The calls drifted close by her, yet quickly receded as if further away. Shaken, she departed from the tour, and had to collect herself in her car before continuing. She later asked if there were any children's groups nearby and was not surprised when the response was no. She could not shake the melancholy until she put some considerable miles between her and the Swamp.

Dr. Hugo Owens asks in his legendary poem, "Lake Drummond":

"What secrets lie buried
Beneath your calm face?
What legends did red men and black
Weave around your dark shores?"

— Davis, 1981

What spirits, magical creatures, beasts, and other secrets are nestled within the impenetrable recesses of the Swamp? The Swamp retains what it wants to keep and has relinquished very little since wood and clothing. Even bones decay at a faster rate due to dampness (most archeological digs yield artifacts such as pottery and bullet casings). There is an abundant supply of folklore about the Swamp; much of it supplied by the locals or "swamp rats," such as the legendary storyteller, Captain Bill Crocket.

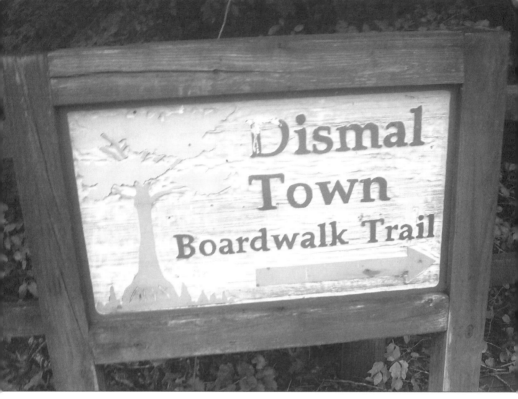

Dismal Town and the Great Dismal Swamp ... people have gone in and not come out.

One mild summer day in July, I visited the refuge, determined to penetrate its thick murkiness. I met with Deloras Freeman, Visitor Service Specialist, who shared some personal insight by describing an experience she had on the boardwalk trail by Washington Ditch on a moonless night. Although a seasoned veteran of the Swamp, she was affected by how *dark* it was.

"Literally, you can't see your feet!" she said. "The forest has such a presence, and in an area so big, you feel the vastness and the lack of human presence."

I agree. Later I went to the very same place, the area of a former camp. I traipsed along the boardwalk, walking through spider web after spider web and batting at the many bugs that droned about my head. I felt both uneasy and in awe of the almost primitive and *thick* forest around me. I felt small. Midway through, I stopped to read a placard explaining about the remains of the camp. As I wiped away the tendrils from a thousand webs off my face, a soft noise suddenly broke my reverie. I looked to my left and beheld a deer in the brush. The doe and I regarded one another, and I wondered just who was the interloper: the deer or me? I pondered the very people who must have felt such trepidation being in the Swamp...the very refuge in which they sought solace. After the deer left, I thought about following it, but I realized how easily I could get lost. You can well imagine being lost in such a forest. You fight panic as you are robbed of your sense of direction because of the thickness of the trees. There have been reports of even the most seasoned sportsman or scout getting lost and being rescued, or never being found at all. Indeed, even Lord Drummond was purported to have gotten lost while hunting — there is disagreement on the accuracy of this record — although he managed to find his way out. Others weren't so lucky.

The Boardwalk that takes you through the forest.

Freeman cautions: "You want to stay on the trails. You can get lost in the forest, and a week later we would never find your body. Nothing remains."

Of course, some purposely lose themselves in the Swamp. Similar to those who had found the Swamp a safe haven from persecution and slavery, there are those who considered it a refuge from misery. There is a story about a young man who lost his girlfriend in a tragic accident near the swamp. They never found her body. For days, he grieved and his despair eventually sank into madness. He was convinced that his lover was still alive. He would tell his friends that her injuries made her wander off into the swamp and he was to rescue her. Even though his friends made every attempt to stop him, he disappeared into the swamp and, despite heroic efforts to find him, he was never seen or heard from again. Locals say that on quiet, moonless nights you can hear him calling for her. Some say his shouts get increasingly desperate, bordering insanity, but as the first light of dawn blushes the eastern horizon his cries of anguish fade into the early morning breeze. In another story, on her wedding day, a patient bride waited for her groom to return from an ill-fated hunting trip, but he never did. That very night, she managed to slip away from her family and went to find him, but she never returned. Every dawn, along the shore of Lake Drummond, her ghost, clad in a luminous wedding dress, appears in the mist, still waiting, still searching. Conversely, Edgar Allan Poe, perhaps so afflicted by despair and addiction, became seduced by the thought of inducing his death by going to the Swamp that he wrote one of his lesser-known poems, "The Lake":

> The which I could not love the less;
> So lovely was the loneliness
> Of a wild lake, with black rock bound.
> And the tall pines that tower'd around.
> But when the night had thrown her pall
> Upon that spot — as upon all,
> And the wind would pass me by
> In its stilly melody,
> My infant spirit would awake
> To the terror of the lone lake.
> Yet that terror was not fright —

But a tremulous delight,
And a feeling undefin'd,
Springing from a darken'd mind.
Death was in that poison'd wave
And in its gulf a fitting grave
For him who thence could solace bring.

This was probably what led noted poet Robert Frost, spurned by his fiancé and saddened by his lack of success, to go into the swamp — to purposely get lost and perish (Franklin, 1979). Determined to end his life, he took a train from Boston to Norfolk, hitched a ride, and then finally hoofed his way to the Swamp. It was quite late when he arrived footsore, tired, and hungry. The night closed in around him. As he slogged through mud and puddles of the unpaved road, catching glimpses of gaslight and other eerie sights of the Swamp, he startled at the occasional animal calls. Frost became so afraid at the idea of spending the night in the wilderness that all thoughts of suicide were quickly dispelled as he realized his predicament. He eventually sought solace by some hunters who kindly took him in for the night. Chastened but wiser by his experience, he returned to Boston, where his fiancée later warmed up to him. His literary career took off as well. In his later years, before his death, he would retell about his venture into the Swamp, thankful that he survived the ordeal.

Like the shelter it promises, the Swamp's dark foreboding wildness is the best place for clandestine love affairs. Another famous story, Lady of the Lake, describes an Indian princess forbidden to love a young brave from a rival tribe. A white canoe was her only means of transportation so they could meet in secret. Unfortunately, a storm had tipped it over one stormy night and caused her to drown. Her lover followed her to the grave by lethal snakebite. Years later, a party of hunters claimed to have seen the eerie sight of a lone white canoe slipping through the murky waters of the lake with two shadowy passengers. Not a sound came from the dipping paddles and no wake marked the water...the canoe then vanished as mysteriously as it appeared. No one could say when the canoe would appear again, but they knew that the passengers were the Indian maiden and her lover, finally together for all of eternity. This sad tale inspired Thomas Moore's ballad "The Lake of the Dismal Swamp."

Standing on the shore of Lake Drummond, near Washington Ditch, I lose myself to my senses: water lapping the rhythms of the lake, smells of water rotting with traces of smoke from the still burning peat fires, the faint chirpings of birds, and the wonderful view of the sky and water. The surface of the lake is brilliantly speckled as a glorious golden path to the sun. However, I can just imagine how my senses, not to mention my imagination, would affect me after the sun went down, as I would be left in the dark...alone.

One canoeist I spoke to loves solitary early evening sojourns along the shores of the lake and described to me how the sound could carry strangely. Being a hundred feet from the shore with no one around, she said, "You hear voices that you know aren't your own." She also related how one evening she saw little bursts of spinning balls of light—a natural phenomenon of swamp gas (a luminescence given off by the decaying of wood or burning methane escaping from decomposing vegetation, or smoldering peat). This can be explained, but it is very disconcerting to see nevertheless. "I wouldn't be caught dead after dark out there. Too spooky," she said.

Other lore that seems to embody the mystery of the Swamp is the white doe. The most famous of all is Virginia Dare, part of the tragedy of the Lost Colony of Roanoke Island, North Carolina. Sallie Southall Cotten depicted the mystery in *The White Doe: The Fate of Virginia Dare* as a lyrical narrative in 1901. Virginia was the first child borne to the colony that Sir Walter Raleigh had established for Queen Elizabeth in 1587, a colony that subsequently vanished. The only remaining clue was the cryptic letters CRO etched in a post. The legend is that after her parents' demise, Chief Manteo of the Croatan adopted the child. When she had blossomed into a young beautiful "pale-face maiden," she became embroiled in love conflict between a handsome young brave Okisko and an evil magician Chico. To keep her to himself, Chico turned her into a white doe, but the sightings of this rare creature caused neighboring tribes to hunt her for a trophy. Alas Okisko, driven to save his fair Winona, as she was called among his people, finally had the means to create a charm to turn her back to her human form. When he finally found her, he administered the charm, but as she was transforming, a chief had simultaneously spied her deer form and let his arrow fly, thus piercing her side. She died in the arms of her lover, and thereafter must haunt the island forever in the form of a white doe.

Actually this motif of the silver deer is very common along the Eastern Seaboard, from Maine to Florida, and can be found nestled in pockets of civilizations all throughout the Swamp thanks to Captain Crocket and his yarning of the tale. The details are similar to those of Virginia Dare, but the significance of the white deer resonates as both phenomenon and the tragedy of ill-fated love. Hunters and biologists have debated about there being an actual white deer in the deer population. Apparently it is a gene anomaly that is quite rare. Despite the fetching price of such a trophy, killing such deer is believed to be a harbinger of bad luck...just seeing one is unsettling enough. Often times the doe has a red mark on its forehead and sometimes it is accompanied by the apparition of a young brave. Those who follow them seldom return, for the spectral lovers lead the unsuspecting further into the Swamp and may encounter a deadly rattlesnake (poisonous snakes are a real threat in the park). The legend has the young maiden initially discovering her lover bitten by a snake and nurses him back to health, which leads to the jealous rival and the tumultuous events that follow. Still those who claimed to have seen just the doe have remarked on how utterly sad its eyes are, as if searching for something or someone and not yet finding it. Others describe the eerie stillness that descends upon them when beholding the spirit doe, as if time had completely stopped. As with any unexplained experience, those who have witnessed such a sight do not wish to speak of it.

If the white doe seems benign and even sad, the Swamp Creature story is the most frightening of all. According to *Myths and Legends of the Great Dismal Swamp* by Hubert Davis, a hunter named Harvey Pruitt saw something so horrible that he was traumatized to the point of speechlessness. Finally Pruitt described a creature "huge as a bear, covered with long black hair" and "ran on its hind feet" (Ibid). It had chased and almost caught him. The next day Pruitt and some other hunters assembled a party to find and catch this hideous creature before any harm befell on the neighboring community. They succeeded on catching it and keeping it in a cage, which drew attention from all over as people flocked to see the beast that walked like a man. It turns out it was actually female! One old-timer had finally traced the child's origins and he described a family who lived in the thickest part of the Swamp. The parents had lost their baby to a she-bear that raised the child as its own. Sadly, despite efforts to civilize the wild child, she died. Or did she? Some claimed she escaped into the night and is still out there. Others say there is a family of hairy beasts preying on small animals.

While some dismiss this as a means to frighten young campers, the tale of the Swamp Creature still exists today, though mostly as urban legend. However, there have been reports of a creature that is similar to Bigfoot. On warm, humid nights, sounds of something crashing through the woods can be heard, and the snarling and growling sounds almost human. Then the shrieks of the beast's fallen prey and sounds of the hapless being devoured follow. By dawn searches typically yield nothing: no tracks, no bones, no blood, nothing remains. Bears might be the culprit, as bear attacks have occurred at the Swamp, but these attacks are very rare. In addition, it's not unusual to hear something large crashing about in the thicket at night. Certainly one can't help but to think of Bigfoot. Can the legendary creature be as far south as the Great Dismal? Perhaps. Or perhaps the Swamp has its own Bigfoot?

The Great Dismal Swamp is a powerful alluring mystery, beckoning us with its lore of bandits, doomed lovers, and phantom deer, and conjuring supernatural beasts to make us doubt our senses while we huddle with fright on those dark nights. It is both shelter and danger. It allows us to consider those brave freedom seekers, who risked life and limb for a better life, and those hardy folk who call the Swamp their home. It is a wild place despite our attempts to civilize it, a stubbornness to be admired. It is truly a place of wonder and beauty.

The Peninsula

Hampton ~ Newport News ~ Yorktown ~ Gloucester ~ Williamsburg

Across the Chesapeake Bay from the Southside is the Peninsula. It is referenced as such because once upon a time the only means of transportation to and from it was by ferry, making it a seemingly distant place indeed. After construction of the Hampton Roads Bridge Tunnel and the Monitor-Merrimac Bridge Tunnel, transportation was easier, thus allowing frequent visits. Known for its many places of interest, the Peninsula is a place worthy of visit. Cities such as Hampton, Newport News, and Yorktown have witnessed the bloody battles of the Revolutionary War and Civil War. These cities are frequently referenced in history books, and many historical sites can be found when touring them.

Chapter Six:

Hampton

Fort Monroe...

Spook Central

Built in 1823, Fort Monroe in Hampton is one of the largest forts in the United States, and its history makes it the most important military structure in the South. Located on Old Point Comfort and built on a man-made island, the Fort was named after the fifth President of the United States and designed by Brigadier General Simon Bernard, the French military engineer and assistant to Napoleon. It was originally built to protect Jamestown and was used to control the coastline during the Civil War. After it was built, it became a popular resort frequented by both political and famous figures. Presidents Andrew Jackson and John Tyler were regular guests to the Fort, staying at the nearby Hygeia Hotel. Gen. Robert E. Lee, second-in-command of the Confederate army, was stationed at Fort Monroe; he later married Mary Anna Randolph Custis, great-granddaughter of Martha Washington, and his son George Washington Custis Lee was born there. In 1861, Fort Monroe was Union occupied, and the fort was used as a transitional place for Confederate soldiers and sympathizers captured by the Union (Quarstein, 1998).

In May of 1862, Abraham Lincoln arrived at Fort Monroe to discuss movement against Norfolk to end the Confederate hold, thus allowing Union control over Hampton Roads and the Peninsula. On May 10, 1865, Confederate President Jefferson Davis was captured in Georgia and transferred to the Fort. He languished there in prison until his release two years later (Ibid).

Apparently a section of the Fort is teeming with so many ghosts that it is called Spook Central. Many historical figures are known to allegedly haunt the Fort. According to the ghost stories, the spirit of Davis haunts Casemate No. 2; however, Davis died in New Orleans and was buried in Richmond. Since it is quite a trek from Richmond to Hampton even for a ghost, this seems implausible, but perhaps the terrible memories of his time spent in prison had affected him so in the afterlife that he remains there in spirit. The former prison also includes ghosts of Confederate soldiers. One ghost materialized before a security guard who had such a fright that he spilled hot coffee all over his lap and didn't even notice.

Robert E. Lee's former house at the Fort is reportedly haunted. Toys have turned on by their own accord, and people have heard heavy footsteps ascending the stairs. Another place, the kitchen, for pots and pans as well as the occupants' nerves rattle. Plates smash to the floor, drawers pull out with utensils scattering about, and cabinet doors open and shut.

At another place, the ghosts apparently do not like flowers. Those who set flowers in vases are destined to wake the next day with petals scattered about like confetti. Another ghost is a little girl. In the basement of one home, residents once found boxes of old discarded toys they didn't realize they had. After they had sealed the box and made preparations to give it to Goodwill, they found the box opened and the toys strewn about. They dutifully packed up the toys again...just to find the box opened and the toys all over. This time they placed the toys in the box and carried it upstairs. As they were shutting the basement door, one heard the muffled laughter of a child.

Another house in Spook Central was the scene of a tragedy. The military wife often has a tough job: mother, caretaker, and mistress of the house. It can be difficult when the spouse is away most of the time. One wife of an officer stationed at the Fort suffered a bad marriage. The husband was prone to anger and tended to be extremely jealous. His wife, understandably, grew increasingly fearful of his temper, and eventually fell in love with another man. Her husband found out. He stole into the house of his wife's lover and shot the couple. To this day, her ghost or, what she is commonly referred to as, the Luminous Lady haunts the alley behind the officer's quarters.

Over time the Fort became one of the most heavily defended in the United States. The Fort's coastal defense during World War II became active again because of the German U-boats that lurked nearby in the Atlantic. Fort Monroe's long history makes it a recognized military installment on the East Coast (U.S. Army, 2009). Today, after the tragic events of 9/11, the Fort is closed to the public. Access to take photographs is limited to the Chamberlin Hotel. Yet the Fort's storied history makes it one of the most interesting places in Hampton Roads.

The Chamberlin Hotel

The Chamberlin Hotel was built on the site of another equally famous hotel—the Hygeia—that once offered elegance and refinement to Fort Monroe in the early nineteenth century. The Hygeia quickly became the choice among the politically powerful and well heeled, for in its time the hotel boasted modern amenities such as an on-site ice plant, laundry, billiard rooms, a bowling alley, and electricity, as well as shops and a telegraph office. The ballroom was renowned for its opulent décor and the dining room had breathtaking views of the Hampton harbor. During the Civil War, the hotel was used for a hospital. It eventually was torn down and replaced by another hotel that burned in 1920. In this spot, the Chamberlin Hotel was built and it closely resembled the Hygeia's highbrow establishment, including a fitness room and an indoor swimming pool (Virginia Historical Society, 2001).

It is because of this fire that most people believe the hotel is haunted. One such ghost is a woman that haunts the eighth floor. She is said to be a young woman named Esmeralda who was married to a poor fisherman. She worked as a chambermaid for the hotel. Life was difficult and often times the family went without food, but their love for one another was very strong. One fateful day her husband never returned from a fishing trip. Every day she waited for him, but he never returned. The manager, angry from finding his employee gazing out the window and not working, fired her. On that very same day a fire broke out in the kitchen and spread quickly to other parts of the hotel. Although most guests were saved from the flames, some weren't, including some of the staff. On the eighth floor, where the smoke was the thickest, her spirit remains. Apparently those who behold her are so frightened that the manager refused to book any rooms on the floor to guests. Witnesses describe feeling cold or seeing the faint figure of a woman glide past them. Others report feeling an intense heat in her presence. Still the reports of a sad woman haunting the halls on the eighth floor are enough for anyone to know why her spirit lingers.

Heightened security and waning business after September 11, 2001 caused the owners of the hotel to go bankrupt despite its popularity for weddings, receptions, and parties. In recent years, the Chamberlain was bought and has subsequently gone through a $54 million renovation as luxury apartments for seniors. Today, the Chamberlin is a beautiful retirement facility that still provides the breathtaking views, the same wonderful dining, and the pleasant breezes from the Chesapeake Bay that made the original hotel so famous.

Chapter Seven:

Newport News

The Boxwood Inn...

A Sweet Spirit

The Boxwood Inn, formerly Lee Hall, has always been a socially oriented place. Simon Curtis, an entrepreneur who helped with the reconstruction after the Civil War, was an ambitious man. The Curtis family's history reaches as far back as the seventeenth century and contributed significantly to Warwick County. Despite his humble beginnings as a maintenance worker at the Lee Hall Train Depot, he was able to amass a small fortune to build the Hall of Records for the citizens of the area. Later, when the Boxwood Inn was built in 1896, he added a post office and a general store. Attached to these busy public places, the Curtis home, which was fronted to both store and post office, was hardly a private residence. Simon Curtis opened his home to many. Every birth, engagement, wedding, and birthday was a joyous occasion. When a glass enclosed porch was added, guests could dance and dine in relative comfort. Simon Curtis and his wife were excellent hosts, and the Curtis family home became the social gathering spot for the well heeled and well dressed.

As the years progressed into the nineteenth century, generation after generation of the Curtis family lived in Lee Hall. Friends and neighbors always commented that it was a house with a great heart as they recalled those fond times. Nannie Elizabeth Wynn was the last of the Curtis family to live there, doing so until her death in the early 1950s. Nannie embodied the Curtis' outgoing and caring spirit, for she continued to invite friends and family over for celebrations despite her frail age. It was as if she continued the Curtis way of giving and sharing. However, as with any old house, maintenance can be quite expensive. After Nannie's death, it was sold repeatedly to several unrelated owners, but then the stately manor house sat empty for a decade during the 1980s.

When I arrived at the Boxwood Inn, I was struck by its antebellum style and beauty. Its two-tiered porch, reminiscent of a past era, causes one to expect to see Scarlett O'Hara leaning over the upper balcony, watching for her Rhett Butler. I can understand why so many brides have their weddings here. I met with the owner Kathy Hulick, who took time out of her very busy schedule (and cleaning) to speak to me about the inn. An energetic woman, she is dedicated not only to maintaining the charming bed and breakfast, but also preserving the gracious Southern hospitality the Curtis family were renowned for. She recently acquired the inn, saving it from those who wanted to raze it to make way for a fast food restaurant. To Kathy it was the quintessential American Dream: an opportunity to build a successful business for herself and her family, and she's doing it quite well. The Boxwood Inn offers a variety of accommodations and entertainment, and is the perfect place for weddings and receptions. Call 757-888-8854 or visit the website: www.boxwood-inn. com for more information.

The Boxwood Inn

The Boxwood Inn also has a special feature. It is haunted. Kathy knew she had inherited a ghost when she took over the inn—Nannie Curtis, or Miss Nannie as she calls her—and felt a profound sense of relief to discover that there were no scary ghosts. At various times Kathy feels Miss Nannie's presence wrap around her like a warm blanket. Miss Nannie is also very rewarding. Kathy remembers times when she has been thinking aloud about budget concerns...and then finding pocket change in the most unusual places. While the discoveries are usually only enough to buy a newspaper or a cup of coffee, Kathy was amused by Miss Nannie's "contributions" to the house.

She remembers one of the first times she saw Miss Nannie's apparition. Running a bed and breakfast is busy work. There is never a lack of anything to do, and she is fortunate to have her family to help her out, including her son Adam, soon-to-be daughter-in-law Bekki, Bekki's brother Adam, her husband Derek, and her sister Jenny. One time, Kathy and her family were gearing the inn up for another occasion. She told Bekki to go upstairs for some clothes while Kathy tidied up the dining room downstairs. There were four other people in the house, but they were in the kitchen cooking. She heard Bekki walking around upstairs. Kathy came around the corner, behind the stairwell, and walked down the entrance hall. She picked up a few things on the stairs to bring upstairs. She looked up just in time to see a figure clad in a long white gown glide past on the upper landing. Heart thudding in her chest, Kathy knew she had seen a ghost, but wanted to make sure she had.

"Bekki, are you walking around upstairs?"

"Yes."

"Did you just walk by?"

A pause... "I'm in the bedroom."

Kathy hurried upstairs. The two searched all around, but did not find anyone who matched the description.

Miss Nannie can be mischievous. One April, when Kathy was in one of the guest rooms cleaning, she tidied up a dress form clad in a nineteenth century nightgown that had been found in the attic. It is the type of old-fashioned nightgown that covered every inch of a woman up to her neck, but charmingly adorned with lace and pearl buttons. Kathy discovered that the gown had been turned around with the front facing the wall. She adjusted it, but later found the same scenario. It was as if someone had picked up the fabric by the shoulders and twisted it around so that the front was facing the wall. Maybe Miss Nannie didn't particularly like the nightgown? Another time, Kathy had been busy with a wedding in one of the dining rooms. She was standing in the entry hallway speaking to one of the guests when she felt the oddest sensation. She felt her hair being plucked. She touched the back of her head. Nothing. Then she felt it again. There were many children scampering about, so she figured it might be one of them tricking her. She looked behind her expecting to find the prankster, but nobody was near. Then she felt it again. Someone or something was plucking her hair!

"I didn't feel scared," Kathy told me. "I knew it was Miss Nannie being playful."

Her family has experienced Miss Nannie too. Kathy recalls a time when her husband ventured downstairs (the family has its private residence upstairs adjacent to the rooms) for a late night snack. While Derek was searching for something to eat, he heard humming and saw something like a white skirt swish by out of the corner of his eye. Kelsey and Kramer, Boxwood Inn's resident cats, have experienced Miss Nannie's ghost, too. One time Bekki witnessed Kelsey getting up on his hind legs as if begging for something. The weirdness of it was that there was nothing there.

Kathy feels that Miss Nannie keeps the house happy as she did in her former life. She is grateful to have such a benign spirit...she only wishes Miss Nannie would help out with the housework!

Chapter Eight

Gloucester

Rosewell Plantation

Built by Mann Page in 1751, Rosewell Plantation was once a stately mansion of Georgian architecture before being gutted by fire in the late nineteenth century. From the wide staircase and the mahogany paneled halls to the Italian marble floors, the house was by far the most luxurious in the area. Thomas Jefferson is said to have stayed here while drafting the *Declaration of Independence*. The Page family is said to have created Virginia's state motto "Sic Semper Tyranus" ("Thus Always to Tyrants") and proposing the charter for the College of William and Mary.

Today all that remains of the once grand mansion is a huge, four-story shell...*and ghosts*. Folks claim sightings of people in period dress descending what was once the stairs and a woman in a red cloak tends to a rose garden. Apparently the ghosts do not take to strangers very well. Visitors (you can only visit during the day) have reported being pushed, feeling sick and dizzy, or feeling as they are moving through pockets of "thick air." Others claimed to have seen a man telling them to leave, but when they come closer, the man disappears. He is described as wearing a uniform, but nothing by today's standards. If you are able to get close enough to recognize it, you will find it to be a Civil War Confederate army uniform!

Chapter Nine:
Williamsburg

Williamsburg is a wonderfully restored eighteenth century town that is rich in America's revolutionary history. It is also teeming with ghosts! You can't spit ten feet in front of you without hitting a nebulous glob of ectoplasm or an anomaly of electromagnetic energy. One summer, weaving our way through the throng of tourists that descend upon Merchant's Square and Duke of Gloucester Street, my friend, Jen, and I encountered the strange side of Williamsburg.

~~~~~

The Peyton Randolph House

The house's history extends back to 1715 with its original owner Peyton Randolph. Generations of Randolphs include various family members who were involved with the House of Burgesses, American Revolutionary War, and the Civil War. As the storm of the Revolutionary War began to darken the horizon, revolutionaries met at this house to debate strategy before continuing on to Philadelphia (Guide, 2007). As with any house of that age, happy events such as weddings, births, and other celebrations are tempered with tragedy. Among the tragic events: in 1824, a child of Mary Monroe Peachy fell from a tree and died from the injuries; many children died there from a host of diseases that were common in that time; and a family member, faced with mounting debt, committed suicide in one of the rooms (Norma and Scott, 1994).

Peyton married Elizabeth Harrison in 1745; a very strong-willed woman, she ran the estate after her husband's death. Some historians paint Elizabeth as a strong and stubborn woman, while others describe her as cruel. Her slave Eve purportedly was the target of her rage. She escaped several times, but she was always taken back to her master who whipped her as punishment. The worse punishment was the sale of Eve, as conditioned in Elizabeth's will, which separated her from her family and home. In the hands of her new master, Eve vowed revenge on anyone who lived in the Peyton home (Behrend, 2000). To this day her vengeful spirit stalks the house. Visitors describe seeing a ghost clad in slaves' clothing appearing in parts of the house. The frightening detail is the ghost's expression of pure hatred. Others claimed to have been wakened to their beds violently shaking.

Peyton Randolph House... On the first floor, in the left furthest window, there seems to be an outline of a figure in the window. Is it a ghost of a woman?

During tours of the house, some tourists report feeling strange in various rooms or the sense of being watched. Others feel an oppressive presence descend upon them in the rear bedroom (Norma, 1994). Tour guides are reluctant to speak about any ghosts that may haunt the house. I approached one tour guide, a young woman sweltering in her colonial costume, and asked her if she had experienced anything. She told me she was not permitted to speak about said ghosts because of LB Taylor and his involvement with the creation of the legendary Tavern Ghost Walk. The ghost stories of Colonial Williamsburg are featured in LB Taylor's *Ghosts of Williamsburg and Nearby Environs.*

"If you want to hear the stories," she said guardedly, "go on the ghost tour!"

I received the same responses from a few other employees. On a personal level, I was at first a little put off by this and fancied the thought of Mr. Taylor holding such sway over the literary world, but then again if employees are forbidden to speak about anything other than the history of the place, far be it for me to distract them from their job. Perhaps the young woman's focus is merely on the historical significance of the house and not the spookiness of it. So Jen and I did go on the tour and I highly recommend it. (Call 1-800-History for more details.)

After the tour, Jen and I were wandering around and came upon the Randolph House. It was late and the house was closed to tours for the day. After most of the tourists have left the square, the silence settles over everything like a funeral pall. There is something so disconcerting about that house at night. The way the streetlights reflect on the windows make them appear to be eyes staring down at you as you pass. We went around the back so that I could take some pictures. As we neared a window on the first floor, I heard, through the window, what sounded like a woman crying. I asked Jen, but she claimed not to hear anything. The house was closed to all visitors at that time and, when I peeked in the window, it was completely dark, but I *heard* the crying as plain as day and I still can't figure out who was causing it. The pictures I took were too grainy and dark to use, but the ones I took during the day of the front of the house came out well. In one there appears to be a young woman pressing her face and hand against the glass. Perhaps it is the condition of the film, or the way light refracted on the glass. Of course, seeing a ghost in a picture these days is akin to finding the likeness of Elvis Presley's face on a cornflake, but I can't help making the connection between the strange crying I heard and this rather woeful woman's face in the picture. Who is the young woman? Perhaps it is Eve... I suppose I might never discover her identity.

A Haunted Bathroom?

This was a very weird experience.

Being late and so very hot due to walking around on a rather humid night, not to mention experiencing an extreme urgency, Jen and I came upon this restroom...totally unaware of it being haunted.

Is this public bathroom haunted? I think so.

I finished up before Jen, washed my hands, and walked out, quickly mentioning to her that I would be waiting outside. At that time I was still reeling from my strange experience at the Randolph House and my nerves were raw. I was exhausted after such a long day. After sitting down on a nearby bench, I heard noises in the men's restroom: sounds of the hand dryers going off and on and someone walking about. I figured it was occupied by someone and nothing more. My friend was feeling the effects of the hot and humid summer evening, so her time spent in the restroom was long. Nobody entered the restrooms; we were the only ones there. Finally my friend emerged and, as she did, we heard all the toilets automatically flush and all the hand dryers turn on simultaneously. Being the braver one, I ventured inside the women's restroom and found all electronics droning relentlessly. I stuck my head in the men's restroom, looked around, and hollered hello, but found no one there. Suddenly everything went quiet. Then, we heard the sounds of someone walking about again and using the hand dryer in the men's restroom. Logically, the phenomena could have been from a variety of causes such as an electronic mishap to overly efficient hand dryers and automatic flushing toilets, but the sounds of footsteps is something I cannot explain.

~~~~~

College of William and Mary

Dating back to the sixteenth century, many ghosts are reputed to haunt this college. One is reported to be a French soldier believed to have died during the Revolutionary War. Others claim it is Sir Christopher Wren, who designed the structure of the school. Faculty and students report hearing heavy footfalls during classes. Perhaps it's Wren, inspecting his work.

Phi Beta Kappa Hall is home to another spirit, Lucinda. Students claim to have seen this apparition appear to them: a young woman with dark hair who wears a white dress. One winter's night, a group of drama students was rehearsing a play. Suddenly they felt a rush of cold damp air. One of them figured someone had opened a door, letting in a draft. It was a cold windy night. Maybe someone left the door open. As the person got up to investigate, he was overcome by a stench of death and decay washing over him. He asked if any of the others had smelled it, but they hadn't. Up in the seats they saw the specter of a woman with dark hair in a white dress. When one turned the lights up, the ghost disappeared (Barefoot, 2004).

Lady Ann Skypwith had a bad temper. Married to a wealthy planter, she was fiercely independent and had a tart tongue. One day, in the late 1780s, she and her husband had a terrible row. In a fit, she stormed out of the room and thundered down the steps. But her heel caught on her dress, and she tumbled to her death. To this day the tread of her footfall can still be heard on the stairwell in Wythe Hall.

Chapter Ten:

Yorktown

Ghostly Remnants of Battle?

The Battle of Yorktown between the Continental Amy, led by General Washington, and the British, led by Major General Charles Cornwallis, began September 28, 1781. This battle was a decisive victory for both the American and French forces. The American army totaled 9,000 soldiers and the French had 7,800. Opposing them was Cornwallis's army of 8,000 (Whitecraft, 2004). October 6 began by the combined forces of the French and American armies bombarding the town with their combined artillery. Incessant shellfire drove townspeople to seek shelter and forced British commander, Lord Cornwallis, to move his headquarters to a nearby cave. By October 17, the British forces were weakened significantly. With little provisions and supplies, Cornwallis realized that surrender was the best option and did so October 19, 1781. The siege had cost the British almost 9,000 men: 556 of them were wounded and more than 2,000 were sick. The Americans had the least casualties with 299 soldiers killed (Ketchum, 2004), but the toll of the battle was not limited to the field; the village of Yorktown suffered terribly.

The townsfolk of Yorktown blessedly heard silence for the first time in three weeks. The booming siege had rattled their town and nerves. News was scarce save for the bits and pieces from soldiers who described trenches, miserable conditions, and small victories (Fleming, 2007). Yorktown was in complete ruin: houses reduced to piles of brick and splintered wood, and the Thomas Nelson home suffered gaping holes in its walls and roof. Citizens picked their way through the still smoking skeletons of their homes and shops, trying to salvage what they could. The injured were carried out on makeshift stretchers to field hospitals. Moans of the dying filled the air with sorrow. Another grim discovery were the slaves the British had amassed as their own with false promises of freedom. Badly abused, ill with disease, or weakened by neglect, they were not high on the list of priority aid and, as a result, quickly died. The ones who survived found themselves in the hands of their new masters, the French (Ketchum, 2004). Yorktown eventually returned to peace, but never to its former glory as a prosperous tobacco port.

Almost a hundred years later, the same battleground was again drenched in soldiers' blood during the Civil War. The Battle of Yorktown was fought from April 5 to May 4, 1862 as part of the Peninsula Campaign. One soldier described his experience: "The earthworks which Washington had built, eighty years before, could be traced as easily as if erected only the day previous, and often times the dirt which had been thrown up by our forefathers to establish the Union was shoveled over by us to perpetuate it" (Dwight, 1989).

The battlegrounds of Yorktown... the fields where ghost soldiers are said to walk.

The cannons at the battlegrounds of Yorktown.

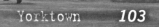

The ramparts at the battlegrounds of Yorktown.

Because thousands of soldiers died, Yorktown is believed to be haunted. Perhaps because of the violence associated with the battle site, those who have witnessed the haunting describe hearing cannon fire, rifles, and the terrible screams of men dying. If you sit by one of the old cannons by moonlight out on the battlefield, you can see soldiers from both wars fighting or walking along.

Cornwallis' Cave is allegedly a hotbed of paranormal activity. However, over the years there has been a decline in EMF readings, perhaps due to the increased traffic of tourists, but recent investigations have yielded EVPs of strange whispers and the soft cries and sobs of the undead.

I didn't see anything.

Cornwallis's Cave

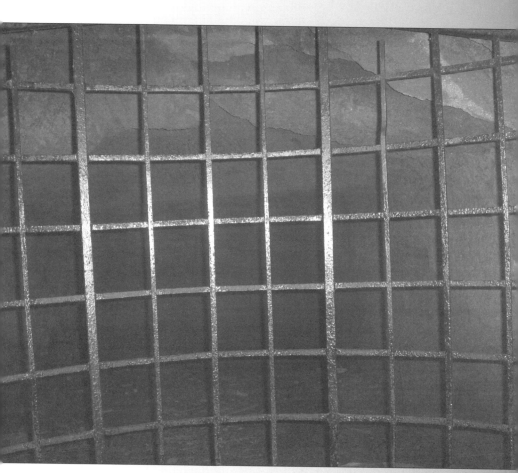

A closer shot of the Cave... note the spookiness!

It was 2:30 in the morning and I was trampling through Yorktown's famous battlefield and being besieged by every manner of flying insect hungry for my blood. I had not dressed properly for this expedition: shorts and a T-shirt. I was very cold and very tired at this point and my shoes were saturated with dew, furthering my misery. I was with a team of ghost hunters, the Lakeland Skeptics Society, and we were to investigate the Yorktown ghosts. However, the only presence I beheld on the battlefield was deer. Their ghostly forms materialized out of the ground fog and watched us warily. Team members Aaron and Kayla diligently measured the site with their equipment while I rubbed my tired feet. I did hear what sounded like cannon fire, but later discovered that the noise was carried over from the late night traffic that was rumbling over the steel lift on the Coleman Bridge, which stretches over the York River. I wanted to see something. I wanted to see the grim countenance of a ghostly Confederate soldier leering at me or the tattered remains of a battle-weary Revolutionary soldier materializing out of thin air, but all I saw was deer.

~~~~~

The Nelson House

The Nelson family and later three generations of the Captain George Preston Blow family made this house their home for over two hundred years. The grandfather Nelson emigrated from England in 1705 and became a prosperous and influential merchant who built the Nelson family business in 1730. His son, William, continued to successfully run the family business and eventually served the community as president of the Governor's Council and as acting governor. Thomas Nelson, Jr. served the public in the Continental Congress, the state legislature, and was governor of Virginia from June through October 1781. He was also a dedicated patriot. Not only did he sign the Declaration of Independence, but he also commanded the Virginia militia at the Siege of Yorktown. He died six years after the war ended (Yorktown Historical Society, 2008).

During the Civil War, this home became, at separate times, a hospital for both Confederate and Union soldiers. It stayed in the Nelson family throughout the nineteenth century until descendants put the home on the market in 1908. In 1914, Captain and Mrs. Blow bought this house and later renovated it. It was then known as York Hall until 1968 when the National Park Service bought it and turned it into a museum.

People have reported seeing soldiers from the Civil War era and hearing the sound of voices within the home. Visitors have described feeling a sudden cold rush of wind in the hallways while others have reported feeling cold spots in the house and feeling watched. At times, the house is reported to shake and sounds of cannon fire from the nearby battlefield can be heard. A cannonball — a gift from Cornwallis's army — is still embedded in the bricks of the outside wall of the house.

As I sat on the backstairs of this house late at night and waited patiently for entities that never revealed themselves to me, ghost investigator Kayla addressed the other realm by asking questions. We peeked in the windows and prowled the grounds, but found nothing that suggested a haunting. Much of the activity, such as noises, was explained by natural causes. The only experience I felt worthy of mentioning is that the batteries in my recorder kept dying and had to be replaced frequently — a known phenomenon in the ghost investigating world.

Alas, besides the EMF meter lighting up like a Christmas tree in the Yorktown cemetery and the constant task of changing the batteries in our equipment, nothing else happened that night. One would assume that the team's labors at Yorktown proved fruitless and my experience was boring. However, there is something eerie in Yorktown, for the stories are perpetuated in many ghost books and on Internet paranormal chat rooms. Past investigations have concluded that Yorktown is haunted.

Ghosts are a fickle lot. They may manifest...or not. Devices can only do so much and, if nothing remotely suggests the slightest twitch on an EMF meter, you wind up empty-handed. Be patient, though. If you ever go on a ghost hunt to Yorktown, be aware that there is no guarantee you will experience a ghost. What you don't see or experience the first time, you may the second or third or even fourth time, and these results may not be evident until you listen to the tapes and view the visuals—a process that can take hours. In addition, as I write this, the team had not finished compiling their findings. Perhaps I did not see anything, but the instruments may sense something else. Yorktown remains worthy of investigation.

Section Three:

Ghosts,
Legends, & Lore

I've included other ghost tales from cities and towns normally not associated with Hampton Roads, but are part of the region. Many of these stories are passed down from generation to generation. The details may have changed over the years, but the familiarity of them still remains. I would even argue that some of the tales have certain recognizable motifs of haunted locales...perfect places for supernatural events to occur, such as the lonely stretch of road on a dark night, the crumbling remains of a once stately mansion, and the thick and seemingly impenetrable spooky forest at midnight. These tales transcend regions and cultures. What has always fascinated me about ghostly lore is that therein exists a system of beliefs whose purpose is to explain either a causal agency between events or morality. Actual ghost sightings can be completely random and may not represent anything (unless a story is associated with the haunting) other than the unexplainable.

However, a ghost tale contains an element of caution. Reckless and irresponsible behavior can only lead to serious consequences, which can be interpreted as the theme of the tale of old Jim who wished to be a fast walker (see A Walker in Windsor). Other tales may cause necessary change. For example, the sighting of the notorious Devil Dog on Shore Drive could serve as a cautionary tale as it can be interpreted as an ill omen. The subtext seems to cry out: there is a dangerous curve in the road. Slow down and perhaps you can avoid seeing the terrifying creature. I can argue that this story causes us to not only test the limits of believability, but also encourages community discourse. Tragic accidents lead to civic meetings that have resulted in heightened awareness, which, in turn, may lead to road improvements. Therefore, these tales embody social awareness, morality, and even a reflection of popular culture —

larger issues that make us question our environment and ourselves. Is it an urban legend or something more implicit such as a commentary on our inconsistent nature? You decide. Shore Drive is a very dangerous road, particularly at night; therefore drivers should be cautioned...lest the Devil Dog be seen!

I have also included a variety of legendary figures in this section. Hampton Roads has, among its citizens, famous figures who have included their own historical significance to the rich history, thus making the area distinct.

Chapter Eleven:

The Haunted Roads of Hampton Roads

Ghosts haunt more than just residences. Sightings of ghosts and other paranormal activity can also occur on roads, streets, and even major thoroughfares.

Deadly Elbow Road

Long, winding Elbow Road spans four miles from Virginia Beach to Chesapeake. It is one of the deadliest thoroughfares in Hampton Roads. There have been more than three hundred reported accidents since 2003, four of them involving fatalities. The road is narrow with drainage ditches on either side along some portions of it, and there is a very sharp elbow curve — hence its name... "Elbow" Road — that marks its most dangerous stretch. Once an unpaved country road, it now is a busy two-lane, and those who live nearby have noticed an increase of traffic over the past five years, perhaps due to the easy access that connects the Beach to the rapidly expanding city of Chesapeake. According to *The Virginian-Pilot* article, "No Elbow Room," this increased traffic has taken a toll on the pavement, causing potholes and crumbling seams and many complaints from motorists. There are no shoulders to protect motorists in case of accident or car failure, and because of the poor drainage the road is prone to black ice and standing water. As one resident who knows of the tragic consequences of the road all too well aptly puts it, "It's a dangerous road. Period." (Saewitz, 2008)

Indeed it is. There have been numerous car accidents that involved injuries, and the list of fatal accidents has unfortunately been growing. Most of the fatalities are caused when the vehicle runs off the road and into the ditch that flank either side of Elbow Road. On June 4, 1994, just after midnight in the 2700 block of Elbow Road, near the Stumpy Lake Golf Course, a late-model Mazda missed a curve and hit a ditch, police said in one article from *The Virginian-Pilot*. An eighteen-year-old girl was sitting in the front passenger seat with her seven-month-old daughter in her lap when the accident occurred. The child was ejected from the car and died at the scene. Another tragedy involved an eighteen-year-old male in 2008; he died from a head injury he suffered after his car overturned into a ditch while rounding the sharp curve. Two other fatal car crashes, which occurred in 2006, have been added to the already bloody reputation of Elbow Road. The mother of one victim sadly surmises, "It's a death trap." (Saewitz, 2008)

The deadly curve on Elbow Road... Stumpy Lake is on the right.

On a recent visit to this infamous road one fine day in May, I drove with more trepidation than usual. Driving southeast, just past Indian River, I prepared myself for the coming sharp right turn indicated by the well-worn sign that cautioned me ahead. There have been nineteen accidents along this curve of road since 2003. Although I handled it well, the oncoming traffic in the opposite lane was nerve-wracking, to say the least. Many motorists as well as those who live on or near that curve have complained about how speed can be a deadly factor. As I cleared the curve, I pulled over in what seems to be the only place for a turnaround. That's where I saw the broken glass. Millions of shards of broken automobile glass glittered on the pavement and explosively migrated outwards as each passing vehicle caused small storms of whirling debris. Perhaps it was because a passing cloud momentarily blocked the sunlight or maybe it was the cool breeze coming off from nearby Stumpy Lake, but I felt suddenly cold. I could almost hear the squeal of brakes and the sickening shudder of colliding metal. I grimaced in reaction to the many tragic accidents that played in my mind's eye. Back in my van, I continued my drive. As I drove further along, I noticed the ditches and how deep they were. What was so disconcerting was the thought of driving on this road at night... one small mishap can easily cause injury or worse.

At night, Elbow Road is even more hazardous as there are few streetlights and it's mostly surrounded by thick trees. "When you have a dangerous road like this, you have ghosts," said one of the men who fished along the bank of Stumpy Lake. He added that this stretch of road is particularly haunted from what he thinks are the result of the fatal car crashes. While there isn't the archetypal "lady in white" ghostly hitchhiker, there are stories of phantoms that roam the road at night. A jogger running with his dog was struck near the curve and his apparition can be seen late at night. There have been sightings of strange lights and ghostly cars. One late night traveler described at what she first perceived as a rude motorist in the opposite lane whose high beams were on and would not turn them off. The lights momentarily blinded her, but, as she passed them, she realized that there was *no car*, just the lights. Sometimes the sounds of an accident, a particularly violent one, can be heard, but when investigating to see if anyone is hurt, no person, living or injured, and no wrecked cars can be found. Some local ghost hunting teams have taken photographs of the road at night and found frightening dark shapes in the trees and floating spectral orbs, indicating paranormal activity. Whatever lurks in the darkness along Elbow Road does not rest easy.

Recently there has been much debate about the mystery surrounding reported sightings of a child's footprints in the dirt by the road around midnight. Some speculate that the footprints belong to a little girl named Annabel who drowned in Stumpy Lake over seventy years ago. A local psychic named Michael Brazell of Soul Interaction Research Team described his experience at Elbow Road: there is a small pump station before the sharp curve in the road, and beside it there is a little cove that Michael and his team beheld a shadowy figure he believes is the little girl. Legend has it Annabel fell off a boat and drowned, but what Michael had discovered — *or rather what the spirit revealed* — is that her father killed her. He described her as very playful ghost who tends to haunt the "safer" section of the road, particularly because of the more malicious ghosts. The little girl even warned Michael to go no further, lest he encounter the "mean ones." Michael believes some of the ghosts of the road harbor a lot of negative energy that feed on people's fears. During one investigation of Elbow Road, in mid-December around midnight, he and his team felt an actual presence coming through the trees, a very hostile one, and the sound of running footsteps coming right at them. He also feels that this negative energy may be the cause of the fatal accidents, considering that the drivers were almost always alone and the time was mostly at night. Michael aptly concludes, "The road has a lot of energy. Be careful when driving on it."

Turning onto Centerville Turnpike, I left Elbow Road behind me, but I couldn't help thinking of the lives lost. Efforts have been made to ensure motorist safety. Both Chesapeake and Virginia Beach have made efforts to decrease traffic, and Chesapeake made the effort to improve drainage by making the ditches even deeper. Virginia Beach has a $44 million plan to replace portions of the two-lane road with a wider four-lane highway and, as of this writing, planned to spend over $800,000 to install a traffic light at the intersection of Elbow and Indian River by the fall of 2009. Plans for Chesapeake to build shoulders, a $5.7 million project, have been temporarily shelved in hopes that the four-lane highway will improve traffic and ease safety concerns. Of course cost is always a factor in civil engineering, but officials hope that these improvements will reduce the number of accidents. Particularly since development in the form of office buildings, strip malls, and even plans for a new high school to be built by the road is increasing due to the ever-growing city of Chesapeake as new neighborhoods are replacing the farmlands. As long as there are those who will continue to use the road, traffic will increase despite efforts to curb it. However, until these improvements are made, Elbow Road remains treacherous.

Eerie Crafford Road

Known to many as Crawford Road, Crafford Road begins off Yorktown Road and ends near the historic triangle of Yorktown. It is a very narrow road, a country lane would be more apt, and has no streetlights, which makes the road very dark at night. It was originally named Crawford Road and that name still appears on Internet maps. Although it does not have the dangerous curve that makes Elbow Road such a caution, it does have a bad reputation. According to Yorktown Police Sergeant Hicky, "It is a very secluded road. Very lonely." This makes it appealing to the daring and reckless. Crafford Road seems to suffer from its own reputation.

While the road is dangerous and secluded, the bridge that marks the intersection where Crafford Road passes beneath Historical Tour Drive bears Crafford Road's eerie reputation. Historically speaking, a crossroads is often associated with evil since it is a place that one direction of energy is crossing over another one going in the opposite direction. This trope is often depicted in literature as the place where wayward people often encounter the devil that bargains for their souls. Many stories about this particular bridge involve an unseen force that can cause your car to break down when parked underneath or nearby. Other tales circulating on the Internet describe bizarre occurrences such as twisting shadows darting across the road, car radios losing transmission signals while going under the bridge, or hearing strange sounds in the forest surrounding the overpass. A story has it that about one hundred years ago, a young woman was set to marry the man of her dreams, but the relationship was a dangerous one at the time because she was African-American and he was white. The details of the story conflict as to whether or not a child was involved, but reach a consensus that the relationship was doomed from the very start, for, on her wedding day, her groom never showed. Speculation is that he was feeling pressure from his family and he vowed, or was forced to vow, to never see her again. Jilted, she walked along Crawford Road (as it was known then) still wearing her wedding dress, wailing over her loss. At that overpass, she hanged herself, though others claim that her death was not by her own hand. If you go to that very same bridge, you might see the spirit lady in white falling and then abruptly stopping in mid-air, swaying to and fro as if being hanged.

Despite its seclusion and violent history, most teenagers find it the perfect place to hang out. It is also a place for teens to prove themselves worthy as they take part in an initiation rite; groups of teens will take a hapless soul to the overpass bridge during the dead of night and leave him or her there to brave the supernatural elements. Those seeking initiation must go up the embankment, cross over the bridge, and back down again. Sounds simple enough; however, because of Crafford Road's notoriety, the worst part is waiting for your friends to come back and pick you up! Before there were cell phones to make the communication easier, initiates had to use Walkie-Talkies. One such initiate, thinking back to her high school years twenty years ago, remembers a terrifying experience. "Ronnie" said the only means of communication she had with her friends was a walkie-talkie so that they could come and pick her up when she had finished. She remembered standing there in the middle of the night, watching her friends drive away and wondering what the hell she was doing out in such a place. She then braced herself for the coming feat. She ran up the embankment, tripping over exposed roots and stumbling over unseen ground as she clambered up the steep hill. It was so dark and disconcerting that she was unable to see where she was going. "That's when I heard the noises."

Is Crafford Road haunted?

She described hearing what sounded like shouts. "It was men shouting and then somebody yelling for help. I heard someone crying...a female crying. And then I heard gunshots and sirens." But she says that the sounds were bouncing all over the place so she couldn't grasp where they were coming from or who was making them. "The shouting became angrier and angrier and real close." She frantically called on the walkie-talkie for her friends, who assured her that they were on their way. As soon as she reached the middle of the bridge on the overpass above Crafford Road (where Historical Tour Drive crosses over), the noises abruptly stopped. The sounds did not fade away, but just stopped as if cut off. Ronnie remembers standing stock still, not daring to move or breathe. Gradually she got her feet moving again. As she completed the rite, she never heard the noises again. When her friends finally picked her up, she was still trembling. She had asked if they saw any police cars or an ambulance, to which they replied no. As they reached the sanctuary of a brightly lit fast food restaurant for much needed refreshment, she realized that the spot where she was on Crafford Road was miles from any major streets, so the sirens would have been heard in the distance... *not up close.* The next day, she paid special attention to the news, but learned no crimes or accidents occurred on or near Crafford Road. "I'll never go there again under any circumstance, and I tell my daughters to steer clear."

As I drove down Crafford Road with nary a car in sight, I couldn't help feeling somewhat vulnerable being on the road alone, not to mention the feeling of claustrophobia because of the dense forest closing in on both sides of me. Although my visit was during the innocence of the day, I can well imagine the creepiness of the night. I finally encountered the infamous bridge and drove under it. I breathed a sigh of relief that my car did not sputter out. I parked it nearby on what little space there was as there are no shoulders, and noticed cigarette butts, empty beer bottles, and fast-food wrappings littering the embankment, which also leads me to believe that this is the ultimate party place. The colorful spray-painted graffiti festooned all over the bridge's surface is a true testament of teenage angst. Other evidence would be the many skid marks on the pavement in various places from, perhaps, drag racing... or could these be the result of cars skidding to a stop due to something in the road? There are rather blatant graffiti messages; some depicted swastikas, KKK, and profanity laden threats.

The claim that Crafford Road is *not* haunted is creating discord among local paranormal investigative teams. Some argue that the rumors are a result of an urban legend gone awry and can find no evidence that suggests a haunting. As for the ghost of the jilted bride, there are no records to validate if such a person hanged herself or was murdered. Others claim that the road is haunted and have pictures of spectral orbs and EVPs to prove it. Locals are wary of any visitors, so I didn't get any information about ghosts — and what I *have* heard tends to darken the already murky character of the road. The road is long and it is very remote, a dangerous place to be in the middle of the night, especially if your car breaks down! The road is not only infamous for its fair share of accidents, but also for death as it has a very violent history. Stolen cars have been recovered on the road, bodies found in the woods nearby, and other crimes such as rapes and carjackings have been reported. However, teenage loitering seems to be the most prominent problem. Sgt. Hicky commented that most of the calls his department receives is typically around Halloween. The police advise any person who does not live in the area to keep away.

Peering through the closeness of the forest on the side of the road, I couldn't shake the feeling of being watched...as if some presence was beholding mine and was waiting for the coming dark to make itself seen. Or maybe it was not a ghost, but a person of flesh and blood—the worst kind! I wasn't about to stick around and find out.

Other Haunted Roads

The Disappearing Man...
Hampton Boulevard, Norfolk

There is a story of a man who walks along the side of the road. He has been described wearing a suit that may date him around the 50s or 60s. People have never really given his features any description because most reports claim his face is almost always in a shadow from the brim of his hat, or that he keeps his head down as he plods along. If anyone stops to offer him a ride or ask directions, he disappears. He remains a mystery, for no one knows his history.

Strange Jackson Road, Suffolk

Over the past seventy-five years, a strange tale of ghost lights has emerged from Suffolk, Virginia. The lights have been described either as oncoming car headlights or a hand-sized green, glowing orb. When approached, it veers off the road and then reappears behind you, or travels down the road and vanishes. Some believe it is the ghost of a railroad worker, waving his lantern to warn others of oncoming trains. Others say the lights are the result of a fatal traffic accident and the vehicle lights are from the deceased's vehicle. Still others claim that it is an extraterrestrial influence. Whatever the reason may be, the lights remain unexplained.

The Devil Dog...
Shore Drive, Virginia Beach

Locals who lived near or on Shore Drive has seen their share of bloody accidents. Paramedics, police, and firefighters have depicted heart-wrenching accounts of finding broken bodies laying crumpled amid wreckage, or having to pull victims out of trees that were caused by high impact collisions (Chewning). Shore Drive is a dangerous road to be sure. It is also a road steeped in mystery. There is an urban legend that still perpetuates to this day of a creature that locals call the Devil Dog. Locals say the creature is mostly seen by the curve and only at night. They describe seeing a black shape darting across the road, a dog with gleaming red eyes, before it vanishes. Still others swear that it's the spirit of a homeless man and his beloved dog who were struck and killed by a car.

Phantom Hitchhiker...
Military Highway, Norfolk

In 1968, during the height of the Vietnam War, a man was drafted into the Army. After he received his orders, he discovered that his girlfriend was not only pregnant, but that she had lost the baby. He was only a teenager, but he tried hitchhiking to the hospital to see her. On the way he was struck by a truck…now those near the intersection of Little Creek and Military Highway have reported seeing his ghost. When someone stops to offer a ride, the ghost vanishes.

Chapter Twelve

Other Haunted Places

Eerie Eastern Shore

Cape Charles

According to reporter Mike Gruss from *The Virginian-Pilot*, a house in Cape Charles in the very southern tip of the Eastern Shore is haunted. In the early 1990s, Mike and Dora Sullivan had a homeowners' dream come true when they purchased a lovely old two-story house dating back almost one hundred years.

Because the house was in dire need of some work, the Sullivans didn't move in right away. Work had to be done to renovate the place upstairs and down. They had discovered that the house had once been a school, a duplex, and then finally sat empty for almost twenty years. As the construction continued, Mike, a retiree, would drop in occasionally to do some of the work himself. One spring afternoon he had been doing work downstairs when he heard a light tapping upstairs. He felt that the sounds were footsteps, but were too light for a man. Thinking it was a building inspector — they can, after all, be women — he investigated, but found no one. No footsteps marked the dust and debris caused by the construction.

The next strange occurrence was the lingering perfume that permeates the house on occasion. Mike admitted that he cannot tolerate strong smells, including perfume, something that his wife has since come to terms with in their marriage. He was alone in the house doing some work when he sniffed the air, catching something floral that floated by like mist. Apparently it was a strong enough scent to cause an allergic reaction. "I hit the wall, and I got this blast of perfume. I had to back away. My nose stuffed up. My eyes were watering."

Mike also found out that it wasn't just him experiencing these un-explainable events...others had too. After the Sullivans moved in, they began experiencing other strange occurrences. Visiting friends and neighbors experienced the same feminine scent of perfume drifting by them as if on the wake of some unseen ghost moving through the room. Lights flickered on and off and the alarm would trigger, although there was no emergency. Even the cat reacted to something mere human senses could not perceive. Most folks in Cape Charles know that the Sullivans' house is haunted. As other incidents occurred that would unsettle even the most skeptical mind, Mike found himself faced with the possibility of sharing his newly acquired residence with a ghost. Something was in the house from another realm, but he and his wife didn't know who it was.

Eventually they discovered the identity of the ghost in question. It is a woman, which they could determine by the perfume, and her name is Sara Doughty. She was a teacher who had taught there when the house was a school from 1912 until her death in 1935. Her haunting is rather benign, according to the Sullivans. Perhaps as a teacher, Doughty insists on order, so she is loath to upset the place. The Sullivans are loath to upset her, for both parties have reached an unspoken truce of living peacefully with one another.

One element of this story intrigues me—the perfume. I wonder if her former students recall her wearing it, and if so, what signature scent did she wear?

Accomack

In the upper reaches of Virginia's Eastern Shore, an archetypal Southern dwelling replete with a wide receiving hall and spectacular views graciously received visitors in its heyday. The Ames were a powerful family, with their children and children's children becoming influential leaders in their community. Alfred Ames became a Methodist minister and his sister Elizabeth married a rector and later settled in Washington, D.C. (du Pont Lee, 1966).

As with any family in the nineteenth century, tragedy often struck the young. Alfred and Elizabeth's older brother, Edmond, became ill from malaria. While Elizabeth did not get sick, Alfred and Edmond did. It was the height of summer and the nursery where the boys were kept was on the top floor of the house. Despite the windows being open, nary a breeze could freshen the cramped quarters. The heat made the boys' fevers worse as they sweated and moaned through their ordeal. At one point, Edmond, the eldest, took young Alfred's hand in his own. He saw his younger brother's sweaty face and his eyes bright with fever and made a decision. "The Lord will take me first." And with this, Edmond lay back on his pillow and died. Alfred recovered from his illness shortly thereafter, but never from his brother's death. Edmond's sacrifice resonated deep within him, said his sister. Years later, days before his own death, Alfred finally told his sister something he swore he'd never tell anybody. Days after telling her about Edmond, he died. His sister Elizabeth died a week later.

Today, little remains of the old plantation. Descendents of the Ames family have pretty much scattered across the region. Yet some say the ghosts of the dead are still seen on the property. Two little boys dressed in nightshirts and holding hands flit across the lawn on a summer's eve and then vanish. Some say on a humid night you can hear the words that echo the grief of Edmond's grave decision. Others say the ghost of an elderly man is seen. He appears to be searching for someone. Could this be Alfred looking for his dead brother's spirit?

~~~~~

Ghosts are Everywhere

Bacon's Castle, Surry

Bacon's Castle, one of the oldest houses in America, was built in 1665 by Arthur Allen. In 1676, it was taken over by Nathaniel Bacon and his men, who rebelled against the governor of Virginia and burned down Jamestown, but eventually Allen did reclaim it. As with any old house, many generations and numerous families have resided there. During the Civil War, the family who had owned the home had slaves who worked in the house and the adjourning fields. An original slave house is still on the property. Several of the windows in the home had initials or names etched into them, including one that had an entire love letter from one of the young owners to his wife. They were a young couple, only married about four years, before she died at the age of twenty.

The house is now a historical site and opened for tours. Rumors persist that it is haunted. Usually the experiences involve the stairs. People claim to have been pushed while ascending or descending the stairs, and there was one report that a person had fallen and was badly injured. There are also reports of those who went on the tour being tripped on the steps or had the distinct feeling of being slightly pushed, which made them trip. On the Internet, there are several videos posted of orbs appearing and floating over the house. One person claimed to have seen a strange apparition, a shadow in the figure of a man, standing near a van. As the van passes him, the figure disappears. None of my friends have confirmed this account or had the experience of being pushed down the steps, which, I imagine, would be pretty scary, but some did feel "weird" at the house or had the sensation of being watched.

Hoping for Peace in Hopewell

In Hopewell, Virginia, there are two dwellings that get little to no peace. One is the Appomattox Manor. The story associated with this house describes a Union soldier who took refuge in the house during the Civil War while the house was a hospital. Later the man was hidden in the basement wall by a doctor and nurse when Confederate soldiers came by searching for Union sympathizers. A doctor and a nurse were arrested. Badly injured, the man had suffered greatly, but apparently nobody knew of his being there. He died a terrible and lonely death. His body wasn't discovered until after the war. By then it was so badly decomposed that his remains were buried in an unmarked grave. However, some say that during the 1950s, a construction team doing renovations to the house found a crumbling skeleton within the walls, although no record of this can be found. Remnants of a tattered Union uniform were also allegedly found. Could this have been the man? Reports of faint scratching and moaning can be heard late at night.

Another house in Hopewell that is haunted is a private residence. The house is said to be over a hundred years old. Apparently, as the story goes, a man, destitute after losing his fortune, shot his family and himself dead one night. The current owners have declined several requests to be interviewed by local papers, but the house has had several owners over a relatively short amount of time. Perhaps it's because of the paranormal activity that has allegedly occurred in the house. Dishes and glasses are said to have crashed to the floor, bed sheets and pillows have been ripped off of sleeping family members, and loud crashes were heard coming from the basement although no source for it was ever found. It is unknown if they have contacted a paranormal team to ascertain the activity. Since it is a private residence, the curious have been turned away, but the haunting has continued.

A Specter in Smithfield

There is a quaint restaurant in Smithfield called Smithfield Station, renowned for its delicious food such as its namesake Smithfield ham and the panoramic views of the Pagan River. The food is so good that it even draws a ghost! According to *The Ghosts of Tidewater and Nearby Environs* by LB Taylor, a ghost of a man appears late at night. He allegedly drowned in the river behind the restaurant. He stays a while, like a lingering diner, and then vanishes by dawn.

Weird Walker in Windsor

This is by far the strangest folklore I've ever come across, but quite entertaining. Jim was a slow man. He wanted to be fast like the errand boys who delivered messages and goods for the local drugstores. He didn't want to ride a bike or run; he wanted to walk, and he wanted to be a fast walker. Folks say that Jim wanted to be a fast walker so that he could make money being a delivery boy. In fact, he wanted this so badly that he sold his soul to the devil. But the devil's deal turned sour. Jim would walk so quickly that no one could see him as he passed by, just a flash, so nobody believed him. People didn't know whether he was coming or going, and pretty soon ran him out of town. Jim realized that he was tricked. In his despair he went into the woods and killed himself and the devil took his soul. But his ghost still remains. All people see of him is a flash and he is gone. If you ever hear a rustle in the woods and see a flash like lightening, that's just Jim taking a walk.

Chapter Thirteen:

The Legends of Hampton Roads

Double, double, toil and trouble;
Fire burn, and cauldron bubble.

— William Shakespeare, "Macbeth"

Grace Sherwood...

The Witch of Pungo

As early as the fourteenth century in Europe, those who accused a person of witchcraft usually did so out of ignorance and prejudice. The victim's accusers believed she was in league with the devil. However, most of the accusations were usually based on highly subjective evidence. By the seventeenth century, a wave of witch hysteria swept over Europe. Thousands of innocent people accused of being witches were tortured into confessing and burned at the stake. Most Europeans carried this fear to the New World. In Salem, Massachusetts, Cotton Mather, grandson and son of two of the most influential Puritans John Cotton and Increase Cotton, felt that the devil's influence threatened the very survival of New England. The Salem Witch Trials in 1692 is a tragic example of how an entire town believed a group of young girls who accused innocent women and men of witchcraft. Whether the townspeople helped create the witch-hunt or were at the mercy of the events is not clear, but the community became entangled in a dark web of jealousy, fear, and superstition. By late September, nineteen men and women were put to death by hanging.

Most visitors don't know the history behind Witchduck Road's name.

Since most of the accused were women, it can be argued that the witch hysteria was a means to control women who threatened the existing economic and social order. The accused oftentimes was an elderly woman who lived alone. She might have displayed independence by handling her estate as well as any man could. She might have raised suspicion because she healed the sick with herbs and tended childbirth as a midwife, as these occupations were steadily being more male dominated. One such victim was Grace Sherwood.

The New England colonies were not the only ones who feared witches. The fear gradually affected the lower ones too, including Virginia Beach's southeastern section of what is now known as Pungo. In the late 1600s there lived a woman named Grace White, the daughter of a carpenter, John White. A striking young woman, she married James Sherwood, a planter. She bore him three healthy sons. Tragically, in her forties, her husband died leaving her with the arduous task of raising her sons while tending their land. Suspicion first reared its ugly head by Grace's attire: she wore pants! She did not remarry after her husband died in 1701 and ran the family farm by herself with her sons' help. Then tough times settled on the colonists as a summer drought followed a harsh winter. Everyone's crops withered and the harvest was meager… everyone's, apparently, except for Grace's. With such ill luck, a scapegoat was necessary.

Ironically, Grace's accusers were men and women she had known most of her life. She had been the one that had soothed their sick children with herbal remedies or assisted their daughters through difficult births. She might have been the one who had offered a bit of sage advice based on the patterns of human behavior coupled with folk medicine to worrisome wives lamenting their husbands' poor appetites. She was the daughter and wife of respected citizens. She was self-proclaimed God-fearing and devoutly religious. Yet, in 1698, John Gisburne accused her of bewitching his hogs and cotton. Anthony Barnes described a weird night of Grace's sneaking into his bedroom and riding his wife around his bedroom like a horse. Upon Barnes's discovery of Grace, he claimed that she had then changed herself into a black cat that shrunk itself small enough to fit a keyhole in order to escape. Grace fought back and countercharged her accusers with slander, which the court found in her favor. Luke Hill, another accuser, and his wife persecuted Grace so that his wife broke into Grace's house and assaulted her. Both were charged and fined. But the flames of hysteria were fanned to the point that everyone thought Grace was guilty of witchcraft despite her protestations of innocence. In March 1706, her body was searched for telltale signs of a witch, teats that her familiar could suckle and/or a mark of the devil. A group of women, one of them, Mrs. Barnes, her accuser, searched her and found what they believed to be this sign, even though it could have been a mole, and other suspicious markings, much to Grace's humiliation. Her house was also searched, although yielded nothing suspicious. Formal charges were pressed and she was summoned to court July 5 (Jameson, 1914).

Her day in court dawned rainy and unseasonable for July. Grace stood before the court dressed in a somber black dress. Although still attractive, her hair, now salt and pepper, was pulled in a tidy bun at the nape of her neck. She appeared wane and haggard, for her ordeal caused her much grief at being separated from her family for so long. The courthouse was overflowing with people eager to witness the proceedings. She narrowed her eyes as she looked at the rapt faces; some she knew, but most of them she did not. The spectators jostled each other and craned their necks for a better view of the "witch who sold herself body and soul to the devil." The whisperings soon turned into hostile threats and condemnations. The din became so loud that the Justice had to shout for order. One after another, her accusers described various experiences that seemed concocted only by vivid imagination. There were no witnesses who had tangible evidence of Grace's being a witch, only suspicion. However, the jury of women who searched Grace's body came forward and delivered their findings: She was a witch because she bore the mark of the devil. A hush descended upon the spectators as Grace voiced her pleas to the court. She did not make any excuses, nor had nothing to say on her behalf except that she was innocent, according to court records. Because of the scant evidence, the Justice ordered Grace to be tried by ducking on July 10.

Water was thought to be a powerful determining factor: it accepts the pure, but repels the unclean. In a ducking, it was thought that if the woman sunk she was innocent since a body of water would not let a witch into its depths, but if she floated she was guilty. She was led out to the western branch of the Lynnhaven River, now called Witchduck Point, by boat while a hostile crowd on the nearby shore chanted, "Duck the witch! Duck the witch!" Again, the Justice demanded a plea of guilt. Again Grace denied the charges and proclaimed her innocence. "Do ye give consent to this ducking?" he asked. She glared at him. "Aye, if it'll clear me of all charges," she defiantly answered. She was then tied cross-bound with her thumbs tied to her big toes and thrown in the river. The crowd silenced as all waited the outcome. Grace floated to the surface. The crowd reacted by gleefully confirming the court's suspicions. Drenched and dripping, Grace was brought to shore and subjected to another humiliating search by "five ancient woman who have all declared on oath" that she bore the markings of a witch. The court placed Grace in iron shackles and led her back to jail. There she remained for eight years. After her release, she returned to her home.

What type of life she returned to one can only wonder. After such an ordeal, how could she return to "normalcy" after neighbors had accused her of witchery? Whenever she went out in public, there were her accusers, grinning at her misfortune, spitting upon her and shouting "witch!" as she tried to maintain her composure and continue on with her business. But she was a diligent woman, and if she expressed her frustration and possibly anger at the injustice of it all, she did so privately. According to court records, she reclaimed her property and became a law-abiding citizen, despite the shame and scorn her neighbors must have heaped on her. She died of natural causes in 1740 at the age of eighty. (Department of Historic Resources, 2002)

Her legend is more colorful. Local folklore, most of it found in *The Witch of Pungo* by Louisa Venable Kyle or passed down generations upon generations of Virginia Beach locals, paints a vivid portrait of a woman scorned. For of all the toils she endured, she certainly made trouble. While most convey the theme of injustice, others perpetuate superstition. In some, she is robbed of dignity and justice and seeks revenge. On the day of her ducking, she allegedly shouted at her accusers, "Before this day be through, you will all get a worse ducking than I!" (Nash, 2009) She then summoned a fierce tempest that made the spectators scatter for shelter from the deluge. In the midst of the howling winds and fierce lightning and thunder, she stood defiantly laughing at them. Another story describes Grace mocking her accusers by escaping from jail. She was discovered sitting by the very spot where she would be ducked! She is described as enjoying a midday meal all the while laughing at her accusers who gathered on the adjacent shore, staring at her in shock. One account includes her in the company of the devil, while others depict her as a sole figure. Perhaps she was surveying the scene beforehand? Even though she was innocent of witchcraft, rumors of her in accordance with the devil continued even after her death. One story describes the moment of her death as a great wind came down from the chimney and blew soot and ash into the room. When the air cleared, mourners discovered the print of a cloven hoof—the devil's footprint. Others claim that a black cat kept sentinel on her grave for weeks on end and hissed at anyone daring to get too close to shoo it away (Kyle, 1973).

If you go to Witchduck Point on a quiet afternoon in July, locals say you can witness the terrible spectacle of her ducking. If you lean into the wind and strain your ears, you can just hear the distant chant of the crowd and Grace's terrible laughter. You may even see her ghost appearing. Locals describe her ghost as peering out into the glimmering surface of the water, saddened by her destiny.

Another legend seems more fitting of her legacy. Grace was a healer who used herbs for holistic medicine. Folks claim she brought rosemary from England by sailing on a boat made of eggshell and returning with the herb—all in a day's time. Today, rosemary grows naturally all over southeastern Virginia.

Grace Sherwood's legacy reverberates through Hampton Roads. Public acknowledgment of the miscarriage of justice in the Sherwood case was made evident recently by Governor Timothy M. Kaine's formal pardon of her. Local historian Belinda Nash tirelessly led this campaign and commissioned a statue erected in Grace's honor in 2006. The life-size statue stands at the busy intersection of aptly named Witchduck Road and Independence Boulevard, near the courthouse where she was tried and a mile away from her ducking site. Coincidently, the statue is on the property of Sentara Bayside Hospital, which Nash felt most appropriate considering Grace was a healer (Batt, 2006). It was July 1, 2009, almost 303 years to the day of her ducking, when I visited her bronzed likeness. In her arms is a basketful of rosemary and herbs, and at her feet perches a curious raccoon—both symbolize her wisdom and respect for nature. I gazed at her features. Her expression seems wistful, almost touched by melancholy, but I beheld the strength in her eyes. Her ordeal I felt was a testament to the long struggle of women. The plaque that bears her pardon reinforces it: "…The fact that woman's equality is constitutionally protected today, and women have the freedom to pursue their hopes and dreams."

As history and legend prove, Grace Sherwood is an important figure, representing the tragic consequences when superstition and rumor go awry. We should all learn from Grace.

Grace Sherwood

Blackbeard

Of all the wonderful treasures Hampton Roads offers, Blackbeard is the most notable.

Blackbeard was the scourge of the Atlantic in the early eighteenth century. The evolution of the pirate has a long and storied history. Pirates pillaged and plundered hapless vessels in the Mediterranean as early as the fifteenth century. During Queen Elizabeth's reign in England, when Spain and England were at war, certain English ships were given the authority to seize and loot enemy ships, yet they were loyal to England and gave a portion of bounty to the government. England's authority knew of the increasingly numerous raids, but with a wink and nod, ignored the pillaging and reaped in the enormous sums. Gradually these privateers, as they were called, became indiscriminate as they plundered all kinds of ships and, rather than giving the government its portion, kept the booty themselves. After the New World was discovered and colonies began to be established in the Caribbean, these seafaring thieves raided ships laden with cargo and became very rich. The raiders would live among the islands of the Caribbean, mixing with the indigenous peoples, and were eventually termed buccaneers by their method of barbecuing (i.e., roasting meat over a boucan-hence the name *buccaneer*). (Konstam, 2006)

One such famous buccaneer is Henry Morgan whose exploits and tales of high adventure made him a legend. Despite the adventure, the life of a privateer was hard: sleeping on the deck, being whipped for the slightest infraction, eating salted pork and drinking rain water as sustenance, living in one's clothes for days upon days, and rarely bathing. Not to mention suffering sexually transmitted diseases from prostitutes, injuries from raids and drunken brawls, the humiliation of being short-changed by greedy captains, and the ever-present danger of sea storms. However, the lure of easy money outweighed the rigors and dangers of a privateer. Both buccaneer and privateer were lucrative occupations that inspired England's lower to middle class young men. One such lad was Edward Teach (Konstam, 2006).

Teach was born in England around 1680 and was quite intelligent. Literacy enabled him to quickly learn navigation, and a strong will and cunning personality made him rise in rank. He heard of the privateers and the fortunes they made and decided that was the life for him. By

1713, privateer raids had increased, becoming bloodier and more ruth-less. The British crown was passed on to those who no longer sanctioned such raids. The line in which the privateer or buccaneer would not cross, the pirate did so willingly...with great relish. Teach was one such captain and, once he crossed the boundary from privateer to pirate, he embarked on a historical life's voyage of greed and destruction.

During the summer of 1717, in the Bahamas, Teach happened upon a glorious opportunity. Major Stede Bonnet was a learned man and his ship, *Queen Anne's Revenge*, was privately owned, with his private quarters stocked with books and fine wines. Bonnet, though, made a poor pirate. After a disastrous attack on a Spanish war ship that caused the deaths of half of his crew, he readily handed his ship over to the ambitious Teach and his men. Over the months, Teach managed to plunder six merchant vessels in the Caribbean, with word of his exploits spreading fast (Parry, 2006). One can just imagine standing on deck and peering through a spyglass that beheld the awful vision of an approaching ship that bore the flapping black flag with the notorious pirate insignia. Such a sight surely struck fear in the hearts of any crew that spotted Teach's ship as it neared.

Seizing a ship had to be a terrifying experience for the victims. The pirates would swarm over the ship, howling like a pack of ravenous dogs. Intimidating with threats, perhaps killing or maiming a victim or two, he and his crew would overtake the ship quickly. Teach believed in ap-pearances and always dressed the part of a menacing pirate. The more his image frightened, the easier it was to prey on ships that displayed little resistance. By 1718, rumors of a "tall Spare Man with a very black beard which he wore very long" eventually became fraught with terrible details as one such captain fearfully recalls:

He wore a sling over his shoulders, with three brace of pistols hang-ing in holsters like bandoliers; and stuck lighted matches under his hat, which appearing on each side of his face, his eyes naturally looking fierce and wild, made him altogether such a figure that imagination cannot form an idea of a fury from Hell to look more frightful. (Parry, 2006)

In time, his legendary black beard, which Teach adorned with braids and ribbons, became his trademark insignia, and he was henceforth called the name Blackbeard. Although evil as some would describe him, he did possess good qualities. For example, despite his brutish ways, he was quite the charmer among the ladies and managed to amass fourteen wives (Konstam, 2006). He was also a good captain to his crew. Loyalty among the crew towards the captain was often the bond that held a ship together (Ibid). To earn their respect, he had to take the most risks, make the crucial decisions, and be braver and stronger than his crew. Blackbeard knew the ever-present threat of mutiny if he did not deliver the goods he promised. Whenever the occasion warranted the crew to indulge themselves in women, drink, and food, Blackbeard came through. He also showed acts of mercy to his captives. He rarely killed; he left that gruesome task to his crew. Yet his fearful reputation preceded him, and as a result, placed a great price on his head.

By the early summer of 1718, Blackbeard had a flotilla of battle-ready ships and a crew of over three hundred men. He even made his way into the Chesapeake Bay, making the early colonies of Norfolk, Virginia Beach, and Portsmouth very nervous indeed (Shomette, 1985). There is a hill in First Landing State Park in Virginia Beach called Blackbeard Hill because its vantage point made spotting ships in Lynnhaven Bay to prey on easier. Lake Joyce is a reservoir that once linked Little Creek to Lynnhaven Bay, and pirates took advantage of this by digging a canal and using the excavated soil for the hill (Squires, 1928). From this vantage point, ships rounding the curve of Cape Henry and entering the Chesapeake Bay would alert Blackbeard to attack. This view on Blackbeard's Island (privately owned) can still be seen today, although the original height has been eroded to a lesser degree (The Beach, 2006).

But even among the most resilient pirates, disease can take its toll. Pockets of Yellow Fever were scattered among the islands of the Caribbean and some of Blackbeard's crew had contracted the disease. He made his way to Charleston, South Carolina, to get medicine. Blackbeard was no fool. Charleston was a bustling port city. Although he desperately needed the medicine for his ailing crew, he was still a pirate. Blocking the harbor, he took advantage of the merchant ships coming into Charleston and plundered nine of them. He held the town for ransom for six days until the governor gave into his demands. He now had more money than ever, but nowhere to spend it. He then set his sights on North Carolina, seeking a less disorganized government.

Image means everything. Blackbeard thought it best to make his image less dangerous, making his devious ways easier. He was pardoned by the governor of North Carolina, Charles Eden, and married the daughter of a wealthy planter, settling into the life of a respectable citizen all the while continuing his clandestine affairs by occasionally plundering local boats and robbing the locals. Since Bath was sparsely populated, perhaps Blackbeard's reputation made him somewhat of a celebrity among the locals, if they didn't fear him. But the sedentary lifestyle in the bucolic surroundings gave way to boredom. After a month, he returned to sea to plunder again, but this time the governor's pardon gave Blackbeard free reign to do what he wanted. This apparently was extended into the Caribbean as he continued to prey upon ships and then bringing the booty back to him to North Carolina to bribe and intimidate officials further (Parry, 2006). Blackbeard seemed untouchable. Perhaps this was his undoing.

In the winter of 1718, the governor of Virginia, Colonel Alexander Spotswood, grew weary by the reports of Blackbeard's exploits and planned to capture him. Piracy can be an ambiguous term. Spotswood was a savvy businessman as he was a shrewd politician. When he discovered Blackbeard so close by, he considered all the political advantages he could gain with Blackbeard's capture, including the pirate's loot. Even though Blackbeard received an official royal pardon, if he surrendered he could keep his fortune. However, if caught in the midst of a plunder, Spotswood would keep a good portion of it, possibly even setting him up. Yet the question remained as how to capture such an elusive figure as Blackbeard? The operation must be a stealthy one.

On Thursday, November 21, the Navy descended upon Blackbeard's sloop the *Adventure* that was located on the western side of Ocracoke Island. On-board a small civilian sloop the *Jane* was Lieutenant Maynard, an experienced naval officer. Two other sloops accompanied his. Under the cover of darkness, the ships bore down upon Blackbeard. As the first wisps of dawn lightened the eastern sky, Blackbeard's crew finally spotted the *Jane* and the alarm sounded all throughout the *Adventure*. Blackbeard, still groggy from the previous night's grog, ascended upon deck to see for himself. Blackbeard had powerful friends and had heard of the attack, so why did he choose to remain in Ocracoke with his enemies bearing down upon him? Perhaps he felt invincible, having warred with the mightiest of ships. The Royal Navy was one more jewel in his crown. Perhaps if he were to engage in battle and win, he could be more powerful than ever.

Except that his once famous flotilla was reduced to the sloop *Adventure* and he had only a third of the crew he had before. For six months he had taken the role of a landlubber as he lavishly indulged in his wealthy lifestyle. He spent a fortune on fine clothes and liquor, gambled, and showered expensive gifts on his many wives. He also became lazy, which made some of his men grow disenchanted with him.

The ships greeted one another with cannon explosions, causing planks to crack and splinter amid a fog of thick acrid smoke. The pirates leapt onto the deck of the *Jane* and engaged the Navy sailors until the deck ran with blood. Blackbeard set his sights on one person, Maynard. With the fury of a charging bull, he ran at the Lieutenant. He and Maynard first exchanged pistol fire at one another, and then hacked at each other with cutlasses. A cut on Blackbeard's neck and shoulder bled profusely. Despite the lethal blow, Blackbeard stood his ground. Peering about him through the smoky haze on the deck, he saw the crumpled bodies of his crewmen. Some were dying, but most were dead; the rest were fleeing by jumping overboard. It was over. The demon that commanded the seas and struck fear in the hearts of ships in the Caribbean was now on the verge of death. What a fitting image, Blackbeard thought, to die in battle. With all his strength he made one last attempt to dispatch Maynard, but the Lieutenant put him out of his misery. His head was severed from his body, and his body was tossed overboard. Legend has it that his body swam around the ship three times, almost in defiance of death, allowing one last horrific sight of the notorious pirate. Blackbeard's head was hung from *Jane's* bowsprit as Maynard made his way to Virginia and then hung from an iron pole somewhere between Newport News and Hampton as a warning to other pirates venturing in the Chesapeake Bay. His skull later became a popular drinking vessel in the taverns of Williamsburg. It eventually disappeared, but resurfaced again in various parts of New England in the early twentieth century until it finally became an exhibit at the Mariner's Museum in Newport News. However, proving it to be the actual skull of Blackbeard has been difficult (Konstam, 2006).

Legends abounded after Blackbeard's death. The most discussed was his treasure; no one, not even his wives, knew where it was buried. Before he died, Blackbeard had proclaimed that no one would know where it was except for himself and the devil (Konstam, 2006). To this day, the treasure has not been recovered. The other was that Blackbeard's ghost is seen where his head was once staked on a pole. Some claim that he appears in full pirate regalia, only that he is missing his head! The persons beholding his frightening specter describe his clutching a bloody cutlass and lunging towards them before disappearing. Others have seen the ghostly form of the pirate's head, eyes blazing red and his features grimaced in the agony of death. The disembodied head dips and bobs along the ground as if searching for its body, according to reports. These sightings are enough to strike fear in the hearts of anyone daring enough to seek out his ghost... Even in death image means everything to Blackbeard.

Dr. Max Madblood...

Mad Scientist Extraordinaire

Ask any Hampton Roads resident over thirty years of age who Doctor Madblood is and most likely he or she will recite those famous words: "Once upon a time, there was a retired mad scientist who lived in a rundown manor house on the edge of Pungo Swamp..." that began each show or would hum the opening bars of the legendary theme song "Green-Eyed Lady" by Sugarloaf. Thirty years ago, Doctor Madblood was *the* show to watch on Saturday nights. Most fans fondly recall sneaking into the living room while the house slept to tune in to the eccentric host and his famous curly mop wig. He and his assorted cast that ranged from a vampire to a wise-cracking disembodied brain kept alive in a bubbling fish tank were as familiar as friends.

Jerry Harrell, Madblood's alter ego, is very much like the character he plays on TV, except for the lab coat and wig, of course. I had a chance to speak him one sunny day. Harrell is a video production manager at Academic Television Services at Old Dominion University in Norfolk. Gregarious and charming, he conveys the same honesty and engaging wit as the legendary host of horror. He described the show's origins. Doctor Madblood began as an idea he had in 1974. At the time he had recently moved from Richmond to Portsmouth to work as an Assistant Production Manager at WAVY Channel 10. After several months, he noticed the lack of local TV entertainment. There were public affairs shows, but he felt that he could provide more. He wanted to combine his talent for entertainment and love of B movies for a late night audience. He didn't want to do the standard vampire hosting from a coffin routine. He wanted a fresher perspective, something like a Jack Benny/ Dr. Frankenstein character, so he came up with the idea of a retired mad scientist who worked part-time creating monsters and cooking up potions. He got together with his partner Mark Young to flesh out the character and the show's theme, and took these ideas to the general manager whose reaction was neutral at best, doubtful at worst. The show's time was critical to get an audience's attention and a comedy at such a late hour would not produce a sizable audience, the manager warned. However, the window for late night comedy was already available by the burgeoning appeal of NBC's runaway success of Saturday Night Live. With expectations low, Doctor Madblood premiered as a holiday special in 1975 on Halloween at 1 a.m., right after SNL. The movie featured was *House of Frankenstein*. The show's effects were low budget and the humor low brow, but, about two o'clock in the morning, the audience's reaction to a trivia question swamping the phone lines was the measure of the show's success. There was indeed a post-SNL audience for such a show at that time, as the high ratings proved. Soon the show became a weekly feature and more characters were added (Madblood, 2009).

Opposite Page:
Doctor Max Madblood.
Courtesy of Jerry Harrell.

The cast of weird characters each had their own quirky charm and created a cult following. Weirdness was the key element of the show, and characters such as Count Lucudra, Kid Exorcist, Dusty the Crop Duster (all played by Mike Arlo), Nurse Patience Dream (Penny Palen), Princess Lygia (Donna Garis), and other oddballs made the show entertaining. The Brain in particular was another brainchild of Harrell's. He wanted a character that represented cutting edge humor by providing cutting remarks despite its miniscule size, a running commentary to the skit. The formula worked. Fans loved to hate the Brain. Harrell finds himself incredibly fortunate to have worked with such talented individuals over the years and to have seen the development of the characters. Every single show was carefully scripted and choreographed, but the skits must appear impromptu (sometimes they were). This was important because every show had to have that freshness or else, argued Harrell, it wouldn't work.

Some members of the original Madblood cast.
Courtesy of Jerry Harrell.

Part of the show's appeal was its relevancy. Since the show featured science fiction and horror films, the demographic were fans of these genres. However, it became so popular because it had such a down home feel. It was aired in Hampton Roads and had local celebrities, such as Mike Arlo, legendary DJ of the rock stations WNOR and later WFOX. Even the commercials shilled familiar businesses and products. Only Hampton Roads residents could understand and appreciate the humor in skits that parodied current events and local news. Usually the show used pop culture references such as the hit movie-of-the-moment. Sometimes the show combined both. One episode featured a spoof of *Star Wars: The Empire Strikes Back* as *The Umpire Strikes Back*, featuring Yokel riding the back of Fluke Streetwalker during the famous Jedi training scene. "I've never seen a planet like this before," says Fluke (Mike Arlo) breathlessly. "It's all marsh and bog and swamp. What do they call it?" Yokel (Craig T. Anderson) quips, "Pungo!"

Says Harrell: "We wanted to tie together major science fiction/fantasy films and local lore and legend." Although shot in a studio, the show's fictional locale is the very real place of Pungo...chosen because thirty years ago Harrell had never heard of it, but liked the name. He describes it as a once very isolated one-intersection type of town (now developed) and unfortunately the brunt of many jokes. Favorite fodder was the report of a Bigfoot sighting. On one show, Madblood worried that one of his monsters from the basement had escaped again. Soon Hampton Roads citizens were talking more about Pungo than Bigfoot being on the loose! Madblood put Pungo firmly in the heads of his viewers, if not imagination.

The show's main feature is, of course, campy sci-fi and so-bad-they're-good horror movies. Some of the movies were cult classics such as "White Zombie," "It: Terror From Outer Space," and "Bride of Dracula." One of the enormous appeals of the show was the relationship between the show and its fans. Some movies were disasters or, as the doctor would succinctly put it, kerstinkers, that Madblood would touch base with the audience. Harrell felt that the more honest he was with viewers the better. One was *The Mole People*. Harrell explains, "We would have fun with the fact that the movie was awful. If the movie was a kerstinker, I would make it clear to the audience that we're all in this together and we'll get through it!" The more the feature film's plot declined in quality, the funnier Madblood and his cohorts' antics became. The skits reflected the plot of the movie. "Rather than making fun of the movie, particularly if it was a classic, we would try to highlight what made it a classic, and then we would make our skit a satire on the basic idea of the film rather than making fun of the movie."

Lastly, the fans make the show. "It's been really nice over the years to have people who have written to me and say, 'When I was a kid, the only thing I asked of my parents was to stay up on Saturday night to watch your show,'" or "'In 1978 I was fourteen years old and I didn't have any friends, but on Saturday night I could hang out with the Madblood gang!'"

Some folks report still seeing strange lights on at Madblood Manor late at night and that Bigfoot is still on the loose in Pungo. Others claim to catch glimpses of Count Lacudra changing into a bat and other misfit monsters coming and going at 13 Idle Hour Road. The show's legacy lives on in a new generation of fans as the original fans watch Madblood, the still snarky Brain, and the cast of colorful characters with their children and grandchildren. The show is now airing on its original day of Saturday, but at an earlier time (for more viewing information and a Madblood tour go to www.madblood.net). Doctor Madblood is a living legend to Hampton Roads. Summing up his career, Harrell reflects: "I did the show because in 1974 local television was almost nonexistent. I do the show now because there still isn't any. It's the opportunity to have fun and include the viewers to have fun with me. Forget about worrying about the economy. Instead watch this! This is so stupid, it's funny! Have fun!" And we did and still do.

Thank you Doctor Madblood for turning *us* on!

Cast of the Madblood today. *Courtesy of Jerry Harrell.*

Urban Legends...

Bigfoot

What's a book about ghosts, legends, and lore without Bigfoot? Tales of this creature exist all over the world and the details are usually similar. I remember watching "documentaries" of Bigfoot sightings as a child and most of them depicted the same grainy footage of a lumbering hairy creature in the thick of some dense northern woods. Huge caster casings of the creature's alleged footprints would be lined up in a laboratory as a man with thick glasses and a lab coat would try to argue the link between species. Bigfoot is immersed in the collective consciousness of popular culture, and it represents the darker side of nature since sightings tend to be in isolated areas of wilderness. However, attacks by Bigfoot are rare. Described as big, hairy, and smelly, Bigfoot's legacy still remains. Though the last official reported sighting was in 1981, there have been others in the Hampton Roads area. In Northwest River Park in Chesapeake, a camper claimed to have seen a Bigfoot like creature. She described it as over six feet tall, quite hairy, and smelly. Park rangers figured the sighting was a bear, a very common occurrence then. However, when they searched the area, they could not locate any bear tracks, but were overwhelmed by an odor similar to a ruptured septic tank or rotting garbage. Other campers claimed that they heard unusual noises during the night and described something crashing about the brush.

Twenty-eight years later, the story still circulates, but instead of one Bigfoot, it is believed that a whole family of the benign critters exists in the protective shelter of the Great Dismal Swamp (see *Chapter Five*). Campers beware!

Chessie...
the Chesapeake Sea Monster

Does Hampton Roads have its own Loch Ness monster? Could be! The Chesapeake Bay is one of the largest estuaries in the United States, which apparently is big enough for a prehistoric beast. Folks compare it to an oversized anaconda and describe it as dark in color. The earliest sightings were in 1936. A military helicopter claimed to have seen an unknown reptilian beast surfacing off the shore of Tangier

Island. Local fishermen have reported seeing a sea serpent as long as thirty feet near Cape Charles. Officials initially scoffed at the notion of something strange and reptilian skulking about the waters, but allegedly grew more concerned as the sightings became more frequent and even documented on videotape.

Forty years ago, a retired government official reported seeing the monster and its brood off shore near Gloucester Point. Witnesses all gave the same description: thirty feet of a sleek, sinewy dark gray creature that he clocked at about seven to eight miles per hour. The offspring of said creature dipped below the surface when they saw the people, but the parent creature kept swimming with its head erect. In 1982, Robert and Karen Frew supposedly videotaped Chessie near Kent Island. The footage depicts something brownish, slimy-looking, but definitely scaly as most sea serpents are often described. This video intrigued the public so much that the Smithsonian held a mini-symposium on the findings. Although officials could not determine the species, they concluded that something was out there. Chessie, as the creature has affectionately been called, has become the legend of Chesapeake Bay.

Apparently the creature migrates, for various people have seen it frequently from May until September. The reports have been conflicting. One false sighting was of a wayward manatee that strayed too far out of its range in the fall of 1994. It was later captured and returned, on a plane, by the United States Coast Guard to Florida. While this beast was tagged and tracked by the U.S. Geological Survey, Chessie remains a mysterious and elusive creature.

If you are planning on swimming in the waters of the Chesapeake Bay, be on the lookout for a serpentine creature named Chessie!

Afterword:
A House on Holly Avenue

It is for personal reasons that I include this house. I lived in this house for six years with my parents before setting off on my own. Although it was sinking into the weak riverside sediment, which made it incline and the floors slightly uneven, my father bought it for the spectacular view of the Elizabeth River in Norfolk. My mother loved it because of the various waterfowl that she befriended, and which subsequently depended upon her daily feedings. They lived in the house for over twenty-five years.

Nobody knew of the tragedy that would come to this house. My mother was a woman passionate about knowledge. She was studying for a doctorate degree while teaching English at Old Dominion University. She was a member of several literary clubs and attended many literary conferences. Her curiosity was as boundless as her energy. She would pore over books every night, often staying up late, and still have the energy to teach freshmen the next day. The house reflected my mother's intellect. My parents' book collection, which I always thought of as moldy, dusty tomes that took up space, lined bookshelves that covered almost every wall in the house, and the collection was still growing. Every table was stacked high with esoteric journals of criticism, rhetoric, and mythology as well as news journals. One newspaper was not enough for my mother. She insisted that my dad subscribe to at least three papers. Pets were also an extension of her nurturing personality. As if five cats were not enough, on occasion she took in orphaned squirrels, opossums, and once even a raccoon kit. She would nurse and release them just to have them come back. She also acquired a few ducks and a whole flock of geese. The backyard was dotted with various feeding stations, and she would lovingly make her rounds to make sure all were fed and content. My mother was the epitome of life itself...that is why it came as such a shock when she suddenly died one bleak November day.

She had been complaining of a headache to my sister who was with her that day. The headache came and went, but increased with intensity to the point that she passed out. In a panic, my sister called the paramedics, who worked on her for fifteen minutes when they arrived. She was transported to a nearby hospital and slipped into a deep coma. Days later she died. My family was devastated, as were her colleagues, friends, and the wide variety of feline and feathered friends she left behind. Shortly after her death, the holidays, a very joyous occasion in my house, were subdued. My father, faced with a sad future of rattling around the house alone, could not bear it any longer and sold the house. My mother's beloved book collection was sold to help defray the moving costs. I was fortunate to procure a few of her favorites.

After my father moved out, I often went to the house to help with the cleaning and packing. It took my sister and I weeks to sort and pack all the stuff my parents owned. My parents were pack rats, and some of the stuff they had kept all these years I had no choice but to throw away. It was a gray winter's day, a few weeks after Christmas, and I was in my mother's old study sorting through her belongings. When I first arrived, I went from room to room, struck by the awful bleakness. I felt as if the house was bereft of its heart. Later in her study, I began packing a box of her books, notebooks, CDs, the stuffed animals her students had given her, and other miscellaneous items such as games, puzzles, and the puppets she made for my kids. At times I would pause over one item, basking in the good memories; other times, I wilted in despair, as an unfinished project of my mother's would remind me of her sudden passing. I heard a sound. It sounded as if someone was walking down the hallway from the kitchen, heading toward the bedrooms. I then heard someone knocking about in my parents' old bedroom. Thinking it was my sister arriving to help, I dismissed the sound. I heard the same noise several times after that. Then I startled at the sound of my cell phone ringing, breaking my silent reverie. It was my sister. I got up warily. If it wasn't my sister I heard... I immediately thought it might be the realtor showing the house, or worse, an intruder. Keeping my sister on the phone, I investigated the sound, but found no one. Yet what was so disconcerting is that I felt such an overwhelming sadness that I had to leave. That night I dreamed of my mother in that house, wandering from room to room, bereft of her things and looking for us. I woke up sobbing. I would have that dream repeatedly.

A year later, my parents' house finally sold. Before the would-be oc-cupants closed, I had managed to visit it one last time. Although I did not hear the noises, I experienced the overwhelming sadness. Months later, I was still haunted by that recurring dream. Because ghosts represent our desires and seem to validate most beliefs about the afterlife, I anguished over the imponderables: Was my mother haunting that house? Could I speak to her? Help her? One day, I had to know. I needed closure. I drove to the house, all the while wondering how I was going to explain this to the owners. When I arrived, I got out of my car, and rang the doorbell. No one was home. I approached a window and peeked in. I gazed at all the strange furnishings…so alien. Even the landscaping was different. Before I was arrested for peeping into windows, I got back in my car. Since I lived a good hour's drive from there, I decided to wait in my car. I was tired, having little sleep the night before, and managed to doze off. When I woke up, I noticed the owner's car was parked in the driveway. I got out of the car, but hesitated. I didn't know what to say to the owner. I decided not to ask, and drove home instead, my spirits low.

Over the months I would have the same vivid dream. Again the painful emptiness of the house, and again my mother trying to find me and not being able to, and again I would wake up crying. Several times I would work up the nerve to speak to the owners, but lost it as soon as I pulled up in front of the house. Perhaps it was because of how different the house appeared, or probably because of how futile the attempt would be. Finally, one night I dreamt of my mother, but instead of experiencing the agony of her trapped inside the house searching for her family, I dreamt that she was surrounded by light. We were hugging, and I felt warm and happy, as safe as when she would kiss me good night when I was a child. Then we parted, and I woke up.

Did my mother's ghost haunt that house? I'll never know, but I feel she is now free.

Bibliography

Aaron. Interview by author, May 30, 2009.

Barefoot, Daniel W. *Haunted Halls of Ivy: Ghosts of Southern Colleges and Universities*. Winston-Salem, Massachusetts: John F. Blair, 2004.

Barrow, Mary Reid. "An Historic Revival After Years Of Neglect, The Ferry Plantation House Will Be Renovated, Preserving 300 Years Of Local History." *The Virginian-Pilot*, 1996.

Batts, Denise Watson. "Statue of Exonerated 'Witch of Pungo' Finds Place to Rest." *The Virginian-Pilot*, July 11, 2006.

Behrend, Jackie Eileen. *The Hauntings of Williamsburg, Yorktown, and Jamestown*. Winston-Salem, North Carolina: J.F. Blair, 1998.

Black, Laurel Johnson. "Beyond the Veil: Writing about the Paranormal in Basic and First-Year Writing courses." *Teaching English in the Two-year College 34.4* (May 2007).

Bland, Simpson. *The Great Dismal: A Carolinian's Swamp Memoir*. Chapel Hill, North Carolina: UNC Press, 1990.

Brazell, Michael. Interview by author, February 2009.

Brogan, Kathleen. *Cultural Haunting: Ghosts and Ethnicity in Recent American Literature*. Charlottesville, Virginia: University Press of Virginia, 1998

Burgess, Dean. Interview by author, May 2009.

Chamberlin Hotel, The: http://www.historicchamberlin.com/index.aspx

Chewning, Alpheus. *Virginia Beach Shipwrecks*. Charleston, South Carolina: History Press, 2008.

Cutchin, Al. Interview by author, May 2009.

Daniels, Marcus. Interview by author, April 2009.

Davis, Hubert J. *Myths and Legends of Great Dismal Swamp*. Richmond, Virginia: Cavalier Press, 1962.

Department of Historic Resources, 2002.

Du Pont-Lee, Marguerite. *Virginia Ghosts And Others*. Richmond, Virginia: William Byrd Press, 1932.

Dwight, Theodore F., editor. *The Military Historical Society of Massachusetts. Campaigns in Virginia 1861-1862*. Wilmington, North Carolina: Broadfoot Publishing Co., 1989.

Fleming, Thomas. *The Perils of Peace: America's Struggle for Survival After Yorktown*. New York, New York: Harper Collins Publishers, Inc., 2007.

Forrest, William S. *The Great Pestilence in Virginia being an Historical Account of the Origin General Character and the Ravages of the Yellow Fever*. New York, New York: Debry & Jackson, 1856.

Foss, William O. *The Norwegian Lady and the Wreck of the Dictator*. Norfolk, Virginia: The Donning Company/Publishers, Inc., 1977.

Franklin, Rosemary F. "Literary Model for Frost's Suicide Attempt in the Dismal Swamp." *American Literature, Vol. 50, No. 4*. January 1979.

Freeman, Deloras. Interview by author, May 2008.

Garrigues III, R. M. LCDR, MSC, USN. "The Serendipitous History of Discovery and Development Surrounding the Hospital Point Area and Its Naval Hospital in Portsmouth (1558-2000)." www.med.navy.mil/sites/nmcp/CommandInfo/Documents/NMCPHistory.pdf.

Gilbert, Lillie, Belinda Nash and Deni Norred-Williams. *Ghosts, Witches & Weird Tales of Virginia Beach*. Virginia Beach, Virginia: Eco Images, 2005.

Gilbert, Lillie and Vickie Shufer. *Wild River Guide to Dismal Swamp Water Trails*. Virginia Beach, Virginia: Eco Images, 2004.

Gille, Frank H., editor. *The Encyclopedia of Virginia, Vol. 1*. St. Clair Shores, Michigan: Somerset Publishers, Inc. 1999.

Gruss, Mike. "In October There Is Always An Old House And A Ghost." *The Virginian-Pilot*, October 25, 2008.

Harper, Raymond L. *A History of Chesapeake, Virginia*. New York, New York: The History Press, 2008.

HaRPS: www.harpsva.com

Harrell, Jerry. Interview by author, June 15, 2009.

History of Chesapeake: www.chesapeake.va.us.net

Holcomb, Richmond C., MD FACS. *A Century with Norfolk Naval Hospital*. Portsmouth, Virginia: Printcraft Publishing Co., 1930.

Hulick, Kathy. Interview by author, May 2009.

James, Kristine. Interview by author, June 19, 2009.

Jameson, J. Granklin, Ph.D., LLD, Litt.D, editor. *Original Narratives of Early American History*. New York, New York: Barnes and Noble Publishers, 1914

Jamestown, Williamsburg, Yorktown: The Official Guide to America's Historic Triangle. Williamsburg, Virginia: The Colonial Williamsburg Foundation, 2007.

Kayla. Interview by author, May 2009.

Ketchum, Richard M. *Victory at Yorktown*. New York, New York: Henry Hold and Co., 2004.

Konstam, Angus. *Blackbeard: America's Notorious Pirate*. Hoboken, New Jersey: John Wiley & Sons, 2006.

Kyle, Louisa Venable. *The Witch of Pungo: and Other Historical Stories of the Early Colonies*. Virginia Beach, Virginia: Four O'clock Publishers, 1973.

Leitner, Doris Kuebler. *Ghost Stories of Olde Towne, Portsmouth, Virginia*. Portsmouth, Virginia: D.K. Leitner, 1995.

Madblood website: www.madblood.net.

Mansfield, Stephen. *Princess Anne County and Virginia Beach: A Pictorial History*. Virginia Beach, Virginia: The Donning Company, 1989.

McNatt, Linda. "Black Confederate Honored In Suffolk." *The Virginian-Pilot*, October 24, 1999.

Nash, Belinda. Interview by author, March 2009.

Norma, Michael and Beth Scott. *Haunted America*. New York, New York: TOR publishing, 1994.

Parry, Dan. *Blackbeard: The Real Pirate of the Caribbean*. New York, New York: Thunder's Mouth Press, 2006.

Pouliot, Julie. Interview by author, May 2008.

Pouliot, Richard A. and Julie J. *Shipwrecks on the Virginia Coast and the Men of the Life-Saving Service*. Centreville, Maryland: Tidewater Publishers, 1986.

Quarstein, John V. *Hampton and Newport News in the Civil War: War Comes to the Peninsula, 2nd edition*. Lynchburg, Virginia: HE Howard, Inc., 1998.

Riddick's Folly website: www.Riddicksfolly.org.

"Ronnie." Interview by author, March 2009.

Saewitz, Mike. "No Elbow Room." *The Virginian-Pilot*, November 7, 2008.

Salmon, Emily J. and John S. Salmon. *Historic Photos of Greater Hampton Roads.* Nashville, Tennessee: Turner Publishing Co., 2007.

Sgt. Hicky. Interview by author, April 2009.

Shomette, Donald G. *Pirates on the Chesapeake: Being a True History of Pirates, Picaroons, and Raiders on Chesapeake Bay.* Centreville, Maryland: Tidewater Publishers, 1985.

Shumate, Corrie. Interview by author, June 2009.

Skylar, Teddy. Interview by author, July 2009.

Smart Region, August 24, 2009. smartregion.org.

Speidell, Phyllis. "Surprise Visitors: Strange Events May Suggest Ghostly Presence at the Suffolk Visitors Center." *The Virginian-Pilot*, October 31, 2003.

Squires, W.H.T. *The Days of Yester-Year in Colony and Commonwealth: A Sketch Book of Virginia.* Portsmouth, Virginia: Printcraft Press, 1928.

"Suffolk's Roots Run Deep in 200-Year-Old Cemetery, State Landmark." *The Virginian-Pilot*, August 19, 2007.

Taylor, LB. *The Ghosts of Tidewater And Nearby Environs.* Williamsburg, Virginia: LB Taylor, 1990.

The Beach: A History of Virginia Beach, Virginia. Virginia Beach, Virginia: Department of Public Libraries, 2006.

U.S. Army IMCOM Northeast Region Headquarters, Ft. Monroe, Virginia, 2009. http://www.monroe.army.mil/Monroe/sites/local/Default.aspx

US Fish and Wildlife Service. Great Dismal Swamp National Refuge, 2004. Accessed at: www.fws.gov.

Uschan, Michael V. *The Working Life: A Civil War Doctor.* New York, New York: Thomson/Gale, 2005.

Virginia Historical Society, May 2001.

Warren, Joshua P. *How to Hunt Ghosts: A Practical Guide*. New York, New York: Simon & Schuster, 2003.

Washington, Vivian. Interview by author, April 2008.

Weinstock, Jeffrey Andrew, ed. *Spectral America: Phantoms and the National Imagination*. Madison, Wisconsin: University of Wisconsin Press/Popular Press, 2004.

Whitecraft, Melissa. *The Surrender at Yorktown*. New York, New York: Children's Press, 2004.

Woodward, Sue. "A Handsome Home, Distinguished Inhabitants." *Suffolk-Nansemond Historical Society, Volume 9, Issue 1*. March 2000.

Woodard, Sue. Interview by author, May 2009.

Yarsinske, Amy Waters. *Virginia Beach: A History of Virginia's Golden Shore*. Charleston, South Carolina: Arcadia Publishing, 2002.

Yorktown Historical Society, 2008

"Yorktown in the Civil War." Accessed at: www.nps.gov/york/historyculture/yorktown-in-the-civil-war.html.

Young, Linda. Interview by author, July 2008.

Zirkle, Keith W. "Ghost-Hunting at the Myers Place." *The Virginian-Pilot*, October 31, 2008.

Index

Accomack, 123
Adam Thoroughgood House, 48

Bacon's Castle, 124
Battlefield (Yorktown), 100
Blackbeard's Point, 138
Boxwood Inn, The, 88
Bruce-Speers House, 50

Cape Charles, 122
Cavalier Hotel, The, 47
Cedar Hill Cemetery, 70
Chamberlin Hotel, The, 86
Chesapeake, 50
Chesapeake Bay, 147
College of William and Mary, 97
Cornwallis Cave, 104
Crafford Road, 114
Crawford Road, 114

Dismal Town, 76

Eastern Shore, 122
Elbow Road, 110

False Cape, 49
Ferry Plantation House, The, 29
Fort Monroe, 84
Freemason Abbey Restaurant, The, 24

Gaffos House, The, 61
Glencoe Inn, 64
Gloucester, 92
Great Bridge, 50
Great Dismal Swamp, The, 73
Grice-Neely House, The, 59

Hampton, 84
Hampton Boulevard, Norfolk, 120
Holly Avenue, 150
Hopewell, 125

Jackson Road, Suffolk, 120

Laurel Cove, 49

Maupin House, 64
Maxwell House, The, 64

Military Highway, Norfolk, 121
Moses Myers House, The, 22

Nelson House, The, 106
Newport News, 88
Norfolk, 22
Norfolk Country Jail, 28

Old Coast Guard Life Saving Station, The, 40
Old Towne District, The, 59

Page House Inn, The, 28
Peninsula, The, 83
Peyton Randolph House, The, 93
Portsmouth, 51
Portsmouth Naval Medical Center, 54
Prentis House, The, 65
Pungo, 127

Riddick's Folly House, 68
Rosewell Plantation, 92

Shore Drive, Virginia Beach, 120
Smithfield, 126
St. Paul's Church, 28
Suffolk, 65

Trinity Episcopal Church, 51

Virginia Beach, 29

Williamsburg, 93
Willoughby Spit, 28
Windsor, 126
Witchduck Road, Virginia Beach, 128

Yorktown, 100

Haunted Virginia: Legends, Myths, and True Tales. Pamela K. Kinney. Like every state in the Union, Virginia has unique myths, legends, and yes, even true stories that sound much like legends, but aren't. Learn about the urban legend of the Bunnyman and what happens to mortals at his Bunnyman Bridge in Clifton at midnight on Halloween. Prepare to discover the myths surrounding Edgar Allan Poe and other famous Virginians. See why Natural Bridge is actually a haunted tourist attraction. And what makes the Great Dismal Swamp so creepy: Is it the ghosts or Bigfoot? Meet the Witch of Pungo in Virginia Beach and find out that Mothman and the Jersey Devil actually visited Virginia. Read Virginian stories of witches, demons, monsters, ghosts, pirates, strange animals, and soldiers from the Civil War. Come visit a most amazing, frightening, and even intriguing Virginia that you never knew existed.

Size: 6" x 9"	45 b/w photos	256pp.
	Index	
ISBN: 978-0-7643-3281-4	soft cover	$14.99

Haunted Finger Lakes. Dwayne Claud. Explore thirteen haunted Finger Lakes of New York State to learn about this supernatural region. Listen to unexplained noises at the Bristol Town Hall, view changing photographs that were taken at Woodlawn Cemetery in Canandaigua, and see a mirror that reflects spirits at John Cuddleback's Antique Store. Meet a woman in white who vanished without a trace at Sonnenberg Gardens, hear a ghost whistling in an empty room at the Woodworth House in Cohocton, and observe a ghostly man and boy who are seen at the Presbyterian Cemetery in Lysander! The haunts await you in the Finger Lakes!

Size: 6" x 9"	37 b/w photos	160pp.
	Index	
ISBN: 978-0-7643-3358-3	soft cover	$14.99

Spooky Creepy Long Island. Scott Lefebvre. Take a tour of the myths, legends, and ghost stories of spirited Long Island, including the infamous Amityville where murder and mayhem shocked a small town; abandoned and haunted lunatic asylums, the historically chilling witchcraft trials, creepy lighthouses, and the many "Mary" hauntings. Shudder as you read over 35 haunting tales of Long Island's supernatural history.

Size: 6" x 9"		128pp.
ISBN: 978-0-7643-2814-5	soft cover	$12.99